RUDOLF STEINER

Ideas for a New Europe

Translation by Johanna Collis. Lectures One to Four are Lectures 9 to 12 in *Die Sendung Michaels*, Dornach 1983, (Bibliography No. GA 194 in the complete German edition of the work of Rudolf Steiner). Lectures Five to Seven are Lectures 16 to 18 in *Geistige und soziale Wandlungen in der Menschheitsentwickelung*, Dornach 1966, (Bibliography No. GA 196).

Lectures One to Four previously appeared in English under the title *The Mysteries of Light, of Space and of the Earth*, Anthroposophic Press, New York & Rudolf Steiner Publishing Company, London 1945.

The translator is grateful for the assistance given by Robin Cook.

The translation has been abridged by Richard G. Seddon.

Edited by Joan M. Thompson.

ISBN Paperback 1 85584 121 5

Typeset by Emset, London NW10
Printed and bound in Great Britain
by WBC Ltd, Bridgend, Mid Glamorgan.

CONTENTS

FOREWORD

Shortly after the end of the First World War two parties of members of the Anthroposophical Society from England visited Dornach in Switzerland to renew contact with Rudolf Steiner, and on each occasion he made a point of adapting his regular lectures specifically to 'our English friends'. The four lectures in December 1919 were published in America in 1945 under the title *The Mysteries of Light, of Space and of the Earth* and have long been out of print. The three given in February 1920 have, surprisingly, never been published in English.

The fundamental thrust of these lectures is, firstly, the urgent need to learn to perceive the realities underlying the phenomena of decadence in public life, and, secondly, the heavy responsibility which lies on the Anglo-American peoples — because they dominate the world by means of economics — to establish a new spiritual life in the form of Anthroposophy which, in turn, depends on the establishing of a threefold social order. A feeling of shame at the misuse of so much intelligence, merely to satisfy physical desires, can provide the starting-point for a process of change.

Rudolf Steiner's radical analysis, based on a remarkably wide sweep of history, is, after 70 years, even more understandable than at the time when it was given, pointing as it does to the demise of the nation state, which we are only now beginning to experience. Many other important themes are covered, such as the renewal of morality through recognizing the dual aspect of evil, and the roles played by the churches and the secret societies.

When Rudolf Steiner edited reports of his lectures for publication he condensed them considerably. His example is here followed, to the extent of eliminating the many repetitions so natural to the spoken word but foreign to the printed page, and some asides to his audience that are likely to be obscure to a modern reader in English. Otherwise his formulation has not been changed. The aim has been to leave the line of thought as clear and direct as possible.

The guidance given to the English visitors so long ago still stands as a challenge to the peoples of the West which has yet to be taken up.

Richard Seddon, Advent 1991

INTRODUCTION

A Vision of Europe

A large proportion of Rudolf Steiner's work was put forward in the form of lectures. He published a fair number of books, too, but we know that he had reservations about the printed page as a means of conveying the spiritual immediacy of his message; he was too aware of the potential gap between the letter and the spirit. This fact probably had its disadvantages, making Steiner's ideas less easy to assimilate for a wide reading public. But as all serious students of his Anthroposophy are aware, it has overriding benefits which far outweigh the daunting impression of row upon row, cycle upon cycle in the *Gesamtausgabe* (the 'Complete Works'). Not only does it retain the sense of presence, of a great man struggling to convey his vision to the souls of his hearers at what he felt was, or could be, a turning-point in modern civilization. It has given us a uniquely organic body of work, ranging widely across the cosmos of ideas yet constantly accommodated to the human span of listening and speaking. It has given us a body of work which is there not only to be studied, but in which one can live.

Both form and content, and the historical setting of his words, are important for understanding these lectures. They were given, mostly, in 1919, just after the horrifying events of the First World War. Steiner's demand for a renewal of the spiritual life does not meet us in some abstract manner — certainly not as a summons away from the immediate problems of the surrounding world. Almost as if from an ark stranded on the Swiss mountains after a chaotic flood, he surveys the ruins that are left of a Europe just beginning to piece itself together, and takes the opportunity to examine 'the great tangle of civilization'. He speaks not without bitter irony at the 'great achievements' of recent times, if they are judged by the number of people murdered. But in an extraordinary way what strikes us even more is the extent to which he does not seem limited by the critical moment at which he speaks. He seems rather to be looking out beyond the present confusion towards the real possibilities of the coming times. That is why his words still touch us directly now.

Of course we notice a certain similarity in the European situation today. And as we propose to put together a new Europe without the scars and divisions of the last half-century we, too, must examine the 'great tangle' of the past with particular urgency. Steiner's values of moral individualism, of the meaning of destiny for individuals and for nations, as well as his complex 'ecological' vision of the living Earth as the world for which we bear spiritual responsibility, have never been more relevant. At the same time, the awareness of the historical process, which still distinguishes Anthroposophy from all the 'alternative' philosophies, is crucial in avoiding the naïve assumption that we can start again from square one with the slate wiped clean. We shall only find the way forward by understanding how we got here. We cannot escape history; but we can change ourselves and our environment by learning about our deeper connection with each other and the cosmos, the meaning of our physical and spiritual evolution. In all these areas, recent ideas are still catching up with the clarity of Steiner's thought long before the issues loomed so frighteningly near as they do now.

The lectures have, at the start, a rather impromptu air. The lecturer finds rather to his surprise that he will be present for a few days longer. Moreover, the proceedings have been hijacked — I do not mean literally, but the situation has been given an unexpected turn by the arrival of a group of friends from England. The lectures are henceforth addressed in a special sense to them. That is why they include some of his most important statements on what he saw as the role of the English (or really of the whole English-speaking world) from the standpoint of spiritual history. But it is vitally important to understand his perspective. He did speak, it is true, of the English and Americans as victors, but not in such a way that this raises them to a position of special importance. Everything depends, he insists, upon what the victors now make of themselves. The context of his words is the return of a group of friends to the life of Europe, a sign of restored normality and co-operation. His message is that everything remains to be done — but not by the English or in England so much as in Europe as a whole, where like everyone else they have an urgent role to play. Accordingly he begins with a sketch of the European situation and an anthroposophical way forward. Immediately, the marvellous building, the Goetheanum which had been worked upon by artists from many countries, even during the war years, takes on the sense not so much of a Noah's ark but of a seed whose inner significance can now germinate and grow.

The impromptu air rapidly dissolves as we become aware of the depth of thought and insight behind the speaker's words. Even some of the touches that we might assume were thrown in for the benefit of the English friends, such as the reference to Milton's *Paradise Lost*, are in fact deeply considered: Before their arrival he had been conducting an extended analysis of the popular 'dualistic' Christianity which blinkered even the imagination of the great English poet. Steiner reaches far back into history for an understanding of the modern consciousness, whose underlying needs were so little met by the external culture of his day. The crisis of civilization is a chance to see life whole once more.

Dualisms of black and white, Heaven and Hell, must be transcended in theory as well as practice, whether they appear in the guise of victor and vanquished, piety on Sundays versus the materialist working week, or in ways of thought — for example, the divorce between the way we think about the natural, external world, which is largely derived from the classical Greek idea of the cosmos as an organized system, and the way we think about the moral world, which is based mainly on the teachings of the Old Testament prophets. The sculptural group which was to have presided over the first Goetheanum, and can still be seen in the second building, enshrines rather the ideal of striving for equilibrium, for the harmonious interaction and resolution of contending forces. That corresponds, as the lecturer points out, neither to the Greeks nor to the Old Testament prophets but to Christianity as a force in spiritual history. That had not been widely understood. Instead, Christianity had been deformed, polarized, made unrecognizable and ineffective by the civilization which had stumbled into the disaster of the War.

Thus the task of the Engish-speaking friends (and of everyone else) is first and foremost to understand the deeper causes of the modern spiritual predicament. The lesson needs to be understood still more today, where we find sweeping alternatives constantly proposed. Nature or holistic awareness is advanced as an escape from the problems of the individualistic modern consciousness; the rediscovery of myth is proposed as a liberation from scientific or historical limitations. But all the resulting movements, like those of the 1960s 'counter-culture', thereby fail to take root in history. Since Steiner's time we have seen a series of cultural oscillations, swinging back and forth from more liberated to more authoritarian, instead of the twentieth-century breakthrough he hoped and worked for.

In fact, the short-term sequel which effectively made impossible

Steiner's hopes was the catastrophe of another World War and a polarization of Europe more devastating than he could have imagined, from which we are only now escaping. The overall identity of Europe disappeared for more than a generation in the almighty dualism of East and West. On that subject, Steiner elsewhere had much to say that now seems prophetic. His study of *The Tension between East and West* stands as a companion-piece in many ways to what he says here about Europe. It is interesting that he regarded both Russia and America as cradles of types of civilization that had as yet scarcely begun to unfold their essential character, whose significance lay in the far future. Perhaps for that very reason they have been liable to grasp at one-sided solutions and instant philosophical remedies. Europe was long submerged, as regards its own deeper identity, by the warring ideologies. But now, as the resulting paranoia fades, we stand once more in a critical position, at a time — the end of the twentieth century — which Steiner again believed would be crucial to man's spiritual evolution. It is all-important that we rise to his challenge to see things whole once more. On that depends, in the end, the emergence of a convincingly European civilization. England and America stand once again in the role of victors, at least of an ideological war. What will we make of ourselves? Will we risk being part of an equilibrium of disparate forces, of a European culture?

In these lectures, Steiner was not lobbying the politicians. He was addressing a group of seekers for a new form of the spiritual life. Christianity had dropped out of the warring world in which they found themselves, at any rate as a spiritual reality in the sense Steiner described. Its outer shell has grown more brittle still in the intervening time. Steiner was attempting above all to bring the real spirit of Christianity back in a form that could deal with the modern individual and his complicated life. As we see some of the social and historical changes he foresaw actually happening, it is still more important to realize that these changes will be meaningless without the inner development and understanding which he asked of us. The fate of the revolutions that created our divided century shows that individual spirits must bring about new forms; outer forms cannot bring about the existence of new people, untrammelled by the conflicts of the past. Steiner addresses us as individuals, and all of us can contribute to the fulfilment of his words.

His approach to the role of the English-speaking peoples is thus precisely not to single us out, but to put us fairly and squarely back in the picture. The open-handed way in which he does so should certainly go some way to correct the impression (unfortunately still too widespread) that his Anthroposophy is culturally as well as linguistically Germanic. These lectures do not show Steiner worrying for an instant about the survival of German culture. They show him only concerned for the emergence of a broader, freer perspective in which all must strive to understand the complex balance of forces which enables cultural life, just as on another level it enables physical life. The unique character of the English-speaking peoples can contribute deeply to that task.

Andrew Welburn
Spring 1992

LECTURE ONE

Dornach, 12 December 1919

A delay of several days in our departure means that I can speak further to you.[1] I am especially pleased about this as it gives me an opportunity to say a number of things to a group of friends from England who have meanwhile arrived. They will have noticed that our Goetheanum building has been making progress during the intervening troubled years, though it remains unfinished. Nevertheless, the spiritual foundations from which it has grown are revealed in what has already been achieved; so too is the way in which it is related to the spiritual movement represented here. This gives me good reason to take it as my starting-point today, especially now that I have this opportunity of speaking to a larger group of our English friends after such a long time.

Those looking at the Goetheanum will notice the specific connection it has with our spiritual movement. Indeed, the building will perhaps even reveal what kind of movement this intends to be. What would have happened if some sectarian movement had felt it necessary to build a centre for its meetings? A building would have been put up in one architectural style or another, and within it, perhaps, there would have been indications, symbolic to a greater or lesser degree, showing what was to take place there, or perhaps a picture here or there pointing out what was to be taught or promoted.

Nothing of the kind, you will have noticed, has happened in our Goetheanum building. The way it has been built shows outwardly that it is for the use of the anthroposophical movement or the Anthroposophical Society. But in addition it stands there showing in every detail that it has been born out of all that our movement intends to place before the world. From the moment it became possible to speak of building a centre, it became necessary to find a style that in every detail gives expression to the spiritual substance flowing through our movement. It would have been unthinkable to build just any house for it. We had to find an architectural style that expresses exactly what is said in every word and in every sentence of our spiritual science based on Anthroposophy.[2]

I am convinced that someone going sufficiently deeply into what can be truly sensed and felt in the shapes and forms found in this building will be able to read in them those things that are otherwise expressed in words. Note, please, that I say: sensed and felt, not artificially construed. The time has come for something new to be brought into human evolution, something that differs from all that has been entering into this evolution since the middle of the fifteenth century.

Over the last three or four centuries, civilized humanity could be said to have arrived at the following situation. External, practical life in its widest extent, strongly mechanized as it has become, now constitutes a realm on its own, monopolized by those who imagine themselves to be practical people. Alongside this external, practical life we have a number of spiritual views, world ideas, philosophies — call them what you will — that have gradually grown to be unsuited to practical life. The feelings and experiences they give human beings hover above practical life. So stark is the difference between these two streams that it is now possible to say that there are no longer any points of contact where they might influence one another. We run our factories, we send our steamships overseas and we make use of our telephones. We do all this by letting life run on automatically, while allowing ourselves to become enmeshed in the mechanics of life. And side by side with this we preach. The traditional denominations preach in churches, the politicians preach in parliaments, various factions in various spheres make demands on behalf of the proletariat or on behalf of women. But if we were to seek the bridge between what we preach and what constitutes our external practical life we would honestly and truthfully have to conclude that there is no such bridge to be found.

Let me mention the following, merely because it demonstrates particularly clearly what I mean. As you know, there are all kinds of secret societies, such as the ordinary Masonic lodges. Here we find the symbolism of the triangle, the compasses, the set-square and suchlike. We even find the frequently-used phrase: The Great Architect of the Universe. What is all this? Looking back at the civilized world in the ninth, tenth, eleventh centuries, when the Masonic lodges were spreading throughout civilization, we find that all the instruments nowadays placed as symbols on the altars of these lodges were then used as tools for building houses and churches, they were used in ordinary practical life. But in the Masonic lodges today, speeches are given about all manner of splendid things that are entirely alien to practical life.

Gradually we have reached a situation in which people work from Monday to Saturday and listen to sermons on Sunday. The two have nothing in common. We have even come to believe that the further our sermons are divorced from practical life the nearer they bring us to the spiritual world. The ordinary world of everyday life has become something second-rate.

So now all kinds of demands are seen to arise from the depths of human beings, but the true nature of these demands is not understood. On the one hand we have those sermons about the goodness of the human being, and about loving everybody, regardless of race, nation or colour. But where is the link between those sermons and all that is going on in external life? Here we receive dividends from our shares and cash them at the bank in accordance with quite other principles. We found theosophical societies, for example, in which we speak about the brotherhood of all mankind, but what we say has not the slightest effect on our ability to control what we set in motion when we invest in shares. Thus our life falls neatly into two entirely separate streams.

Let me give you an example taken from life. A lady told me of an approach made to her for a contribution to something which in turn might encourage the drinking of alcohol. She asked me: As a theosophist, how can I make such a contribution? I had to reply: Do you have any idea how many breweries have been founded and maintained from the capital invested for your pension?

In the sense of what is truly important we cannot preach, on the one hand, in order to give our souls pleasurable feelings of satisfaction, while on the other we continue to lead our ordinary lives in a routine that has become established over the last three or four centuries. Yet because of the dualism that has come to exist between everyday life and what we might call our spiritual aims, few people have the slightest inclination to go more deeply into this fundamental problem. Today, when they speak of the spirit, most people mean something totally abstract and unfitted for this world, and not something that can make an impact on everyday life.

The question, the problem, indicated by this must be tackled at its root. If we had acted here on this hill in accordance with the aims of the last three or four centuries, we would perhaps have turned to any architect — a famous one — and had a nice building put up here; and in it we would have spoken about things that suited it just about as much as all the beautiful sermons given today suit external practical life. But this was impossible, because this is not the meaning of a spiritual science that takes its orientation from Anthroposophy. From the beginning the intention was different.

When are we justified in speaking of spirit? We speak truthfully of spirit when we regard it as the creator of matter. The most atrocious way of speaking about spirit is to speak of it as living in Cloud-cuckoo-land, where it shall not be defiled by contact with matter. This is quite wrong. We must speak of spirit in a way that describes it as being strong enough to immerse itself in matter. And when we speak of spiritual science it must not be as of something that merely rises above nature, but as a fully-fledged natural science. We must mean that spirit with which human beings can unite themselves, and for which they can be intermediaries when it wants to interweave with social life. A spirit spoken about only in drawing rooms, a spirit to which obeisance is made by being good and by loving one's brother, a spirit that disdains any contact with ordinary life — such a spirit is not true spirit. Such a spirit is an abstraction thought up by human beings, and to devote oneself to such a spirit is not to reach true spirit but to foster the ultimate emanation of materialism.

Therefore we were obliged to raise a building in which the thought, the vision for every detail, comes from what also otherwise lives in our spiritual science of Anthroposophy. It is out of the same context that in these troubled times we have treated the social question on the basis of this spiritual science, which from the beginning of its work has wanted to be the opposite of sectarian, to interpret and serve the great demands being made by our time. Without a doubt there is much in this building that has not succeeded. But immediate success is not what is important just now. What is important is that a beginning should be made in certain things, a necessary beginning. As the nutshell fits the nut and is moulded to its contours, so will every single line, every single form and colour in this building fit what flows through our spiritual movement.

It is so very necessary for this intention to be understood at least by a certain number of people, for the most important thing is this intention, this will.

Let me return to some of the characteristic features that have emerged during the evolution of civilized humanity over the last three or four centuries, features that express the deeper reasons for what is now being taken to absurd extremes in human life. Today many human souls are asleep, deeply asleep, and meanwhile many things are going on that are the absolute opposite of civilized life; they are symptomatic of what cannot but continue to spread more and more. People are living with their souls apart from the most important events of the day. Unless they are directly touched by these events, they live their ordinary lives without being aware of what is actually happening. Yet the actual impetus for these occurrences lies in the depths of people's subconscious or unconscious soul life.

The polarity between spirit and matter that I described earlier is founded on another dualism, one that is expressed, for example, in Milton's *Paradise Lost*. It pervades the whole of modern thought, modern feeling and experience, and modern will. In recent human consciousness there has arisen the sense of a contrast between heaven and hell, or what some call spirit and matter. The difference between the heaven and hell of the peasant in his fields and the matter and spirit of today's so-called enlightened philosophers is merely one of degree. The actual polarity is that of God and the Devil, of paradise and hell. People are sure that paradise is good, and that it is terrible that human beings have moved out of paradise. Paradise has been lost and must be found again, and the Devil is a terrible adversary who opposes all the powers that we connect with the concept of paradise.

Without an understanding of the way soul polarities work right into the furthest reaches of our social laws and social longings it is impossible to imagine the extent of the impact of this dualism. We have to speak in paradoxes nowadays if we want to express the truth — something it is scarcely possible to do without this truth appearing as madness to many of our contemporaries. But just as, in the Pauline sense, human wisdom can appear as foolishness before God,[3] so may the wisdom of people today appear as madness in the future. People have gradually dreamt themselves into such a polarity between earth and paradise that they have come to equate paradise with the divine towards which human beings are expected to strive. They fail to realize that it is as catastrophic for human beings to strive towards this paradise, wanting it more than anything else, as it would be for them to strive towards the opposite. For in imagining the structure of the world to be that which underlies Milton's *Paradise Lost* we are, actually, giving a power detrimental to mankind — if it is striven for one-sidedly — the name of a power that is divine and good for mankind, and we are placing this power in opposition to something that is, in fact, not its true opposite at all. We are placing it in opposition to the Devil, seen as something which is in opposition to the good in mankind.

Our protest against this view is to be embodied in the statue that will be placed in the east of our building, a 9½-metre-high group carved in wood.[4] Here, in place of the opposition between God and the Devil, will be placed what must come to be the foundation of man's consciousness in the future: the trinity of the luciferic, the Christ-like, and the ahrimanic.

In recent civilization there has been very little awareness of this. We have called this building the 'Goetheanum' because it is founded on the Goethean view of art and science. Yet in his *Faust* even Goethe embodies the selfsame error as that described in Milton's *Paradise Lost* when he depicts the opposition between the powers of good and the powers of Mephistopheles. Goethe has created a motley mixture of luciferic and ahrimanic principles in Mephistopheles, combining in him two spiritual individualities in an unnatural way.

We must come to realize that the true image of the human being is one of balance. On the one hand man is tempted to float upwards, striving to lose himself in dreams and fantasies, in false mysticism, in anything fantastical. This is the one power. The other drags man downwards into materialism, into matter-of-fact aridity. A true understanding of the human being shows him to be striving for a balance between Ahriman on one side of the scales and Lucifer on the other.

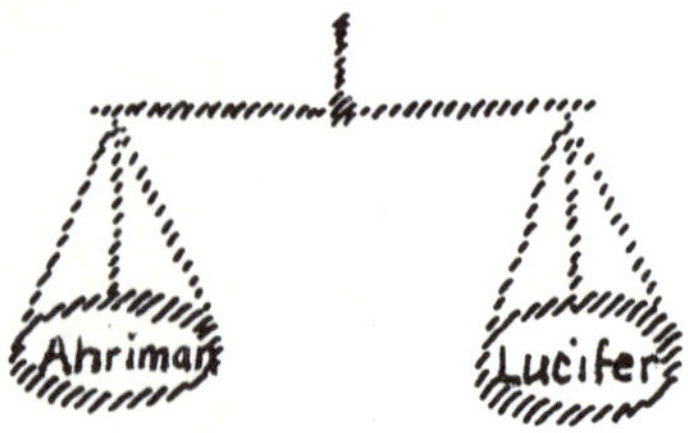

Human beings are faced with the constant struggle of maintaining a balance between something seeking to lead them up out of themselves and something seeking to draw them down below themselves. Modern civilization, however, has come to confuse the dreamy, fantastical nature of Lucifer with God. Thus, when paradise is described, a luciferic picture is painted, and the terrible mistake is made of confusing the luciferic with the divine, because people no longer realize how essential it is to keep the balance between two powers that drag man in opposite directions.

The first thing we must do is to bring this fact out into the open. Strange things are often meant nowadays when the term 'Christian' is used. But the time has come for us to understand that to strive for something Christian means to strive for a balance between luciferic and ahrimanic powers. And we must realize that the last three or four centuries have shut out a true knowledge of the human being to such a degree that little is known of this balance, so that Lucifer has been given the name of God in a lost paradise and Ahriman, who is no longer a proper Ahriman, has become a modern devil, modern materialism or something similar. The real dualism between Lucifer and Ahriman has turned into a fallacious dualism of God and the Devil. The paradise that has been lost is, in fact, a new name for the lost realm of Lucifer.

It is necessary to put things forward in such stark terms today because people must come to realize what a slippery slope they are on, even though this slippery slope is a historical necessity — for necessities are there so that they may be understood. Only the most radical cure will serve to reverse the trend. Very often nowadays the spiritual world is described in terms of something supernatural that does not live here on the earth. People want to escape in spiritual visions from what surrounds us here on our earth, yet do not realize that they are not finding the spirit at all, but the region of Lucifer. So much of what calls itself mysticism or theosophy today is a search for the region of Lucifer. This is because, today, knowledge — in isolation — of something spiritual cannot provide a foundation for people's spiritual striving.

The question that ought to occur to us when we turn our attention to spiritual worlds is: Why are we born out of the spiritual worlds into this physical world? The answer is that there are things to be experienced here on earth which cannot be experienced in the spiritual worlds, and we have to carry the results of these experiences up into the spiritual worlds. In order to achieve this, we have to immerse ourselves in this physical world, and we have to do so with our spirit, in full knowledge. For the sake of the spiritual world we have to immerse ourselves in this physical world.

In order to make plain what I want to say, let us imagine a person leading an ordinary life but having, at the same time, spiritual interests, even exalted spiritual interests. He does all manner of things in order to find out what goes on in the spiritual worlds. He knows intimately everything that is stated in esoteric literature of one kind or another, but for the rest he lives his life in the usual way. All the knowledge he acquires in the course of his exalted spiritual interests is something that can afford him some inner psychological satisfaction — indeed a really luciferic enjoyment — but not one bit of it is carried beyond the gate of death.

There are plenty of people who have a theoretical knowledge of the astral and etheric bodies, but haven't the faintest idea of what happens when a candle burns, or of the miraculous feats involved in making a tram run. They may know plenty about karma and reincarnation, but don't have the slightest idea what is talked about and striven for at a trade union meeting. They're not interested. They are only interested in what the etheric body looks like or what the astral body looks like, and not, for example, in the progress made by capitalism since it became a dominant force at the beginning of the nineteenth century. This knowledge about the etheric body or the astral body is of no use to people once they are dead. All this knowledge only comes to have any value if it is made into a tool with which to enter fully into material life and to absorb here what must be carried over into the spiritual world.

Today all the various branches of natural science are taught at our universities, experiments are made, research is carried out and so forth. And with this natural science we serve our technology, we heal people and do all kinds of things. Side by side with this run the various denominations of the church. Have you ever listened to the content of an ordinary Sunday sermon on the kingdom of Christ and suchlike? What is the connection between natural science and the content of such a sermon? In general — none. The two run parallel. Those on the one side believe they are empowered to speak about God or the Holy Spirit. Even though they maintain that they do feel these things, they speak in abstractions. Those on the other side speak of a nature that is devoid of spirit. Is it right to speak of a Creator in terms that describe some wonderful, interesting spirit who would, however, never have been capable of creating the world? The spiritual powers spoken about so often today would never have been capable of creating the world, because the thoughts we conjure up about them are not even able to encompass our knowledge about nature or our knowledge about the life of human society.

Let me, without being immodest, use an example to describe what I mean. In one of my last books *Von Seelenrätseln*[5] and also often in lectures, I have pointed out the nonsense taught today in physiology about there being two types of nerves in the human body, motor nerves that are the basis of the will, and sensory nerves that are the basis of perceptions and sensations. There is, in actual fact, no difference between motor nerves and sensory nerves. It is simply that what are called motor nerves are there so that we can become aware of our limbs when we make movements.[6]

I merely wish to illustrate how we have natural science on the one hand, and on the other hand all the talk and preaching about spiritual worlds, talk which entirely fails to enter into the physical world around us. What we really need is a knowledge of the spirit that is strong enough to become a natural science. And this we shall only achieve if we take account of the will to which I wanted to draw your attention today. We had to build our building out of the very will of spiritual science. Even the details in this building will come to show that certain important principles can indeed be restored to their proper, healthy basis, though as yet they are still seen in an entirely false light because of the various dualisms we have been talking about. Let me point out one such detail to you.

Look at the series of seven columns standing on either side of our main building. Each column is surmounted by a capital and stands on a base. These are not identical, since each develops out of the one that has gone before. You can arrive at a picture of the second capital if you enter in a living way into the forms of the first and bring thoughts to life within you of how organic forms metamorphose. Your thoughts have to be so alive — and not abstract — that they follow the process of growth. Then you can see the second capital evolving from the first, the third from the second and the fourth from the third, right up to the seventh. The endeavour has been to achieve the living metamorphosis of one capital or portion of architrave into the next — a reliving of the creative activity of the spirit in nature itself. I have the feeling that none of these capitals could be any different.

Something very remarkable has emerged from this. Evolution is usually taken to mean a development from something less perfect to something more perfect and more differentiated, in such a way that the more perfect things are also the more complicated ones. But when I arrived at the fourth capital, it turned out — when I had the fifth to develop from it into something even more perfect — that this fourth capital was the most complicated of the seven. Unlike Haeckel or Darwin, who followed a sequence of abstractions in thought only, I was forced to make the fifth form less complicated, more simple, than the fourth, though the surfaces had to be even more artistic. The sixth was simpler still, and the seventh even more so. I thus discovered that evolution does not denote a development into ever greater differentiation (the straight line is drawn on the blackboard), but rather an ascent to a higher point followed by a descent into something more and more simple.

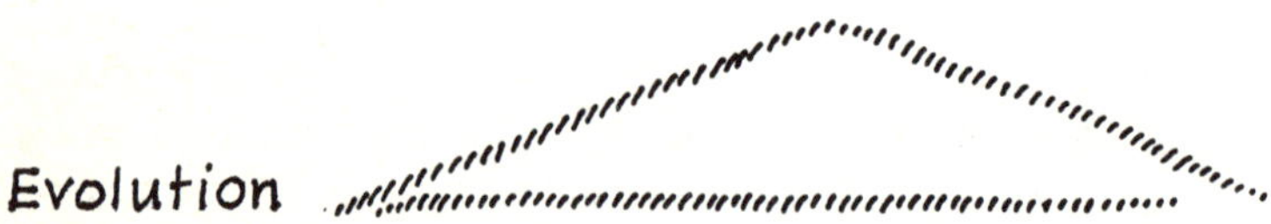

This arose quite simply as I worked. And I saw that this principle of evolution arising in the course of artistic work is the same as the principle of evolution in nature.

Look, for example, at the human eye, which is certainly more perfect than that of many animals. Yet the eyes of many animals are more complicated than human eyes. Inside them are certain blood-filled organs, the 'ensiform process', for example, or the 'fan', which are absent in human eyes, or, you could say, have been dissolved. The human eye has evolved further to something more simplified than some animal eyes. The most perfect is not the most complicated, for it is simpler than the phase in the middle.

Thus, in working this out artistically, it was a matter of following an inner necessity. Our endeavour here was not to carry out research into something, but to shape the forms in such a way that the shaping itself would contain the same forces as those which the spirit of nature lays at the foundation of nature. We seek for a spirit that is creative and lives in the products of this world, and does not merely preach. This is the most essential thing. There is not a single symbol in this building. It is filled with forms that have been taken from the way the spirit creates in nature.

Here we have the beginning of a will that must now find a way to continue. It is to be hoped that in particular there will be an understanding for this search for the very sources of human intention and human creativity, so necessary now in every realm of modern human life. We are surrounded by individual demands arising from the various realms of life. But we also need a summary, a bringing-together. This cannot come from anything floating about in the environment of external, visible existence, for everything visible is founded on something invisible. It is this that we must seek to comprehend today.

I want to urge you to listen intently to what is happening today, and you will find that it is not at all absurd to state that the old is in a state of collapse. But something must be there to take its place. A certain amount of courage is needed to face up to this thought, and this courage cannot be won in external life but only in one's inmost being. It takes courage, for example, to recognize that however admirable the works of Raphael or Leonardo might have been in their own time, to paint today as they did then would be inappropriate. Similarly, the theorem of Pythagoras belonged to its time, and its discovery today would have no cultural significance. Everything belongs to its own time, and things must be understood out of the time to which they belong.

Today more is needed than many people wish to muster, even when they join some spiritual movement or other. We need to realize that we must face up to a new phase in human evolution. Every age is a time of transition, but what matters is knowing what it is that is making the transition. Again and again it is stated that nature and life do not make any jumps. It sounds so wise. But nature does make jumps, constantly.

Step by step nature forms the green leaf proper, then the sepals of the calyx, which are a different kind of leaf, then the coloured petals, which are yet another kind of leaf, and then stamen and pistil. Nature constantly makes jumps as it forms the various structures; and life in the wider sense constantly produces convolutions. In the life of a human being we see an entirely new situation arising at the change of teeth, and again at puberty. And if modern man's powers of observation were more refined, we would also see a third situation arising around the twentieth year, and others after that, again and again.

History itself is also an organism, and it, too, makes jumps. But we pass them by without noticing. People today have no awareness of the significant jump that took place in the middle of the fifteenth century. Yet something that was initiated then is striving to be fulfilled in the middle of our own century. The events that are moving mankind so deeply, and that have reached such a culmination recently, are leading the way to something which is preparing to burst in on human evolution in the middle of this century. These are the things that must concern those who do not want to set up some arbitrary ideal for human evolution but who, with the creative forces of the world, want to discover spiritual science which can then flow into life.

LECTURE TWO

Dornach, 13 December 1919

Yesterday I especially wanted to point out that the connection between this building and our spiritual science is nothing external, but that the ruling spirit of our spiritual science has flowed into the forms in a way that makes possible an important statement: A genuine, sensitive understanding of these forms amounts to a reading of the inner meaning present in our movement.

Looking at the building, you will see that its plan consists of two intersecting circles, one smaller and one larger, like this in a diagram.

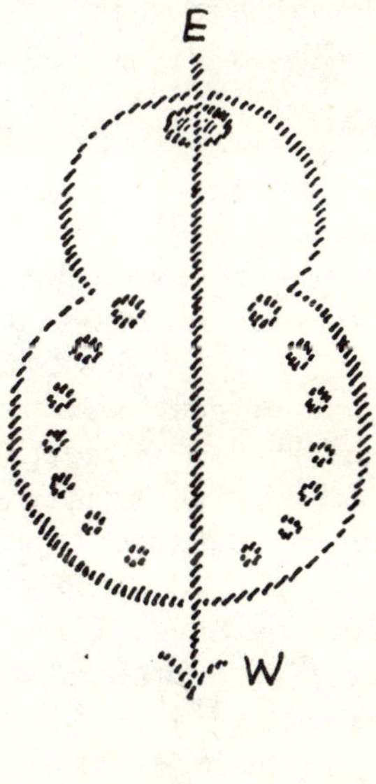

The building as a whole is oriented from East to West. This is the only axis of symmetry, and everything is related symmetrically to this axis. Furthermore, there is no merely mechanical repetition of forms such as that usually found in architecture, where capitals, for example, tend to be identical. There is an evolution of forms in which later ones emerge from earlier ones. Seven columns on the right and seven on the left form the boundary to the side aisles and, as I mentioned yesterday, these seven columns have capitals and bases, and architraves above, that develop their forms in a continuous process of evolution.

If you are sensitive to this plan, really sensitive, you will feel that there is something in these two intersecting circles that points to the evolution of mankind. As I said yesterday, a very important turning point occurred in human evolution around the middle of the fifteenth century. The psychological state and mood of soul in human beings before that time differed entirely from what then began to evolve. And now, in the present, we are in the midst of a development that we can only comprehend if we become aware that we are going towards the future with our own forces of soul, and that the forces of soul that underwent development up to the fifteenth century, though they still haunt human souls, are fading. They are going under; they are doomed to fall away from human evolution. If we want to gain the capacity to have a say in human affairs in the near future we shall have to develop an awareness of this important turning-point in mankind's evolution.

Such matters find their expression in the way human beings want to interpret how they feel and experience things. We need only remind ourselves of one particular aspect of architecture as an illustration of how human evolution moves forward. Look at the forms found in a Greek temple and try to understand them. All the forms in a Greek temple would be meaningless if it were not seen as the shelter, the dwelling place of the god or goddess whose statue is found within.

Proceeding to the next significant architectural form, we come to the Gothic cathedral. You fail to understand the forms of the Gothic cathedral if you can enter it and have the feeling that it is something complete and finished. Just as the Greek temple is incomplete without the statue of the god, so is the Gothic cathedral only finished when the congregation gathers within it, when it is full of people who are listening to the spoken word, so that the spirit of the word holds sway over the congregation, or in the hearts of the congregation. Then the Gothic cathedral is complete, while without the congregation its forms are incomprehensible.

What is it that took place in the evolution from the Greek temple to the Gothic cathedral? In the culture of the Greeks — that flower of the fourth post-Atlantean epoch — there was still a remnant in people's consciousness of the time when divine, spiritual beings lived amongst human beings, only now people felt the need to build dwellings for their gods, because they could only sense their presence in the statues. The Greek temple was the dwelling house of the god or goddess, and people were aware that these beings were present among them.

Then, during the eighth, ninth, tenth centuries AD, we come into the forms of Gothic architecture, which require the presence of the congregation. Consciousness of the immediate presence of divine, spiritual powers no longer existed, for they had moved far away into the beyond. The earthly realm was very much maligned as something that had fallen away from the divine, spiritual powers, something from which to turn away one's glance — which ought to be directed, instead, to the spiritual powers. As though seeking the group spirit of mankind, the individual, in the fellowship of the congregation, sought the power of the spirit, which thus gained a certain abstractness of character. That is why Gothic forms make an abstract, mathematical impression in comparison with the more dynamic forms of Greek architecture.

In Gothic forms everything sweeps upwards, everything points to spiritual distances where the soul must seek what will quench its thirst. For the Greeks, the god and goddess were immediately present; with the ears of their soul they heard them whisper to them. But in the Gothic age the yearning soul could only have presentiments of the divine in forms leading upwards. Human beings built their hopes on yearnings and on searchings, and believed that in these searchings they could be happier within the fellowship of the congregation. They were convinced that what they recognized to be the divine spirit was not something that lived and moved among human beings, but was hidden away in mysterious depths. The expression for this whole mood of soul at that time was the Gothic cathedral, with all its typical forms.

But looking in those days, with their spiritual eyes, at something for which they yearned as the most exalted Mystery of all, human beings had to make the transition from Gothic forms to something that brought together not just the physical congregation, but the whole spirit of mankind in its longing for unity — or all the soul-spirits of mankind longing for a central point and striving towards this mysterious central point.

Imagine the totality of human souls streaming towards each other from every earthly direction of the compass, until all the human beings of the earth unite on this earth as though in a great cathedral — but not a Gothic cathedral, although its purpose would be the same. Imagine in the manner of that time how the seventy-two apostles of Christ were seen to spread out in every direction, planting in souls the spirit that was to stream together in the Mystery of Christ. In what streamed back from every direction out of those into whose souls the apostles had planted the Christ-Spirit, you have — most comprehensively and universally — what the people of the early Middle Ages thought of as something striving towards the Mystery.

There is no need for me to draw all the seventy-two, but I can indicate them. (See drawing.) From these seventy-two columns the rays would stream inwards, coming from mankind as a whole and going towards the Mystery of Christ. Now we can enclose the whole within a wall with a circular plan, and you have before you a cathedral embracing the whole of mankind. Imagine its orientation to be from East to West. The main axes of orientation in a building like this would have to take the shape of a cross, and the main aisles would follow this cross-shape.

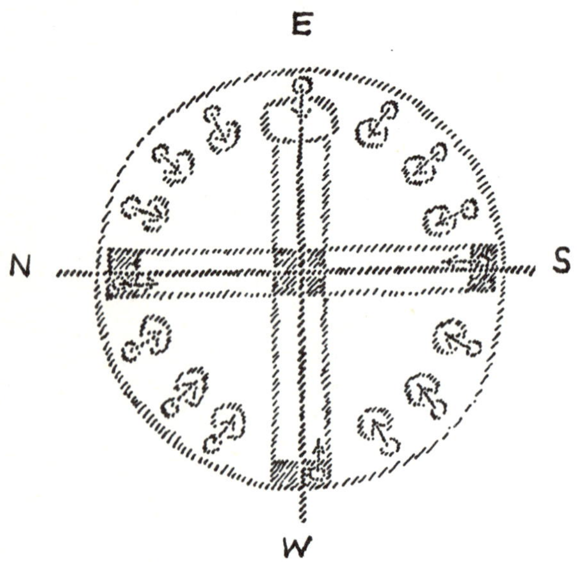

This is how people in the Middle Ages imagined their ideal cathedral to be. There would be doors in the north, south and west; here in the east would be a main altar, and at every column would be a side altar. And where the beams of the cross intersect would have to stand the temple of the temple, the cathedral of the cathedral. Here would stand the summing-up of the whole building, a miniature repetition of the whole. In modern, abstract parlance we would say that a pyx or casket for the sacrament would stand here, and it would have the same shape as the whole building.

The sketch I have drawn is a sketch of the Grail temple as imagined by the people of the Middle Ages, a Grail temple that was the architectural ideal towards the end of the fourth post-Atlantean epoch. It is the cathedral into which streamed the yearnings of all mankind for Christ. In another way, the yearnings of the members of the congregation streamed into the individual Gothic cathedral. It was the house that in all its forms expressed the gathering-place in which individuals tuned their souls to the divine and the spiritual. That is why, in the centre of what I might call the 'archetypal temple' of the end of the fourth post-Atlantean epoch, there stood the temple of the temple, the cathedral of the cathedral. Of this as a whole it was possible to say: When we enter here we can raise ourselves to the mysteries of the universe! The cathedral was a building you had to enter. The Greek temple was a building about which you merely had to say: This is Apollo's house, this is Pallas Athene's house. But the middle point of that archetypal temple, that mid-point where the beams of the cross intersect, made space for the Holy Grail; this is where it was kept.

In this way we have to seek out the moods that are characteristic of the different periods in history. Unless we do this, we do not discover what actually happened. And, most important of all, without such considerations we cannot come to understand the soul forces that are coming into play in our own present day.

People in the Middle Ages, who sensed the earthly world to have been deserted by God, by the divine, longed to find their way to the gods, or to God. Now, though, we stand at a new beginning, for only a few centuries have so far passed since the great turning-point in the middle of the fifteenth century. Most people do not see what is coming into being, but something is indeed coming into being, and things will be different for human souls. These things cannot be intellectually thought out in theory; they can only be sensed, felt, seen with artistic eyes, and those who want to bring them down to abstract concepts fail, in fact, to understand them. But it is possible to indicate these things in various ways.

Let us say again: The Greeks felt the god or the goddess to be a contemporary, a fellow citizen. Medieval people had the cathedral that was, in a way, a door to the path leading towards the divine. People gathered in the cathedral and sought God from the basis of the group soul of mankind. It is characteristic of the Middle Ages that people at that time had something that can only be understood as belonging to the souls as a group, for until the middle of the fifteenth century the individual human being did not play such an important role as has since been the case.

Since then the most essential aspect of human beings has been their endeavour to gather together the strength of an individual personality, to find a mid-point in themselves. All the social demands of our time are incomprehensible without an understanding of the way in which the spirit of individuality is coming into play in every single human being, so that every individual now wants to stand firmly on the foundation of his or her own being.

As a consequence of this, something is becoming extremely important for us in this age, which began in the middle of the fifteenth century and will not draw to a close until we approach the fourth millennium. When we say that every human being is striving for his own particular individuality, we are, in fact, expressing something undefinable. It is much easier to understand what is meant by the group spirit, even if it is a group spirit of a small group, than it is to fathom what every human being is searching for at the source of his own individuality. That is why it is extremely important for people today to understand what is meant by the search for balance between two opposing poles.

One of these poles goes off into flights of fancy. In it lies everything that makes people become dreamers full of fantastic ideas and delusions, filling them with vague, mystical stirrings towards some indefinable infinity. The other extreme — to put it simply, but none the less truthfully, having regard to the spirit of our present age — is the pole of matter-of-factness and arid dullness, the pole of philistine values and bourgeois narrow-mindedness, the pole that drags us down to the earth and into materialism. These two opposing forces exist within individuals. Between these forces stands the human being who is faced with having to find a balance. But there are many ways of finding a balance. Whether you put fifty grams or fifty kilograms on the one side, and the same on the other, the scales are in balance; and they are also in balance if you put one kilogram on either side, or one thousand. There are infinite possibilities for making the scales balance. Correspondingly, there are infinite possibilities for being a human individual, and that is why it is so essential today for people to understand that their individual being arises from their endeavour to seek a balance between the opposing poles.

For the ancient Greeks it was important to feel that in their community Pallas Athene or Apollo ruled, and that this is Pallas Athene's house, and that is Apollo's house. It was equally important for medieval people to know that there was a gathering place that perhaps contained a relic of a saint, or even the Holy Grail itself, a place where they could gather and in which the yearnings of their souls could stream together towards a shrouded Mystery. And it is just as important for the people of today to develop a sense of what they are as individuals, a sense of the fact that as individual human beings they are seekers after balance between two opposing, polar forces.

Psychologically this can be expressed in terms that describe how, on the one hand, something makes people have flights of fancy, makes them dreamers with fantastic ideas, and causes them to develop feelings of desire and pleasure without any regard for the realities of existence. The other extreme, in psychological terms, is what draws them towards the earth, towards matter-of-factness and intellectual aridity. Expressed in physiological terms you could say that the one pole is everything to do with the heated blood, which becomes feverish if it is overheated, while the other is everything connected with boniness and petrification in the human being, which, if taken to extremes, would lead to the various forms of sclerosis. We are psychologically healthy when we find the balance between a dreamy, fantastical attitude and a matter-of-fact, philistine attitude. And we are physiologically healthy when we can live in balance between fever and sclerosis. This can be achieved in an infinite variety of ways, and it is in this that the individuality can live.

This is what man today must feel to be the meaning of Apollo's words: 'O man, know thyself.' They do not mean 'know thyself' in some kind of abstract way. They mean: 'Know thyself in thy striving towards balance.' That is why we must put, in the east of our building, the statue that will help human beings to sense this striving for balance and in which the central figure is the figure of Christ. The endeavour has been to depict this figure in such a way that one can imagine how Christ really moved upon the earth in Palestine in the human being Jesus of Nazareth at the beginning of our era. Conventional depictions of a bearded Christ are creations of the fifth or sixth century, and they are definitely not what one might call true to life. Here the endeavour has been made to create a picture that is true to life and shows Christ as the representative of the human being who is searching and striving for balance. (See drawing.)

In this group you will see two figures: here Lucifer plunging down, and here Lucifer striving upwards. And down here, linked, in a way, with Lucifer, an ahrimanic figure, and here a second ahrimanic figure. And standing in their midst the Representative of Mankind, placed between the Ahriman figure of philistine, matter-of-fact, arid materialism and the Lucifer figure of dreamy, fantastical unreality. The Ahriman figure shows everything that leads human beings to petrification, to sclerosis. The Lucifer figure shows everything that leads them feverishly beyond the limit of what can healthily be tolerated.

In the middle of our way to this point we had the Gothic cathedral, which contained relics of saints, or even the Holy Grail — something not connected with beings actually walking about here on earth. And now, today, we have returned, in a way, to a building that envelops something, but what it now envelops is the being of man in his striving for balance.

If destiny so wills that this building shall one day be completed, those who sit down within it will see before their eyes the Being who gives meaning to earthly evolution, and seeing this Being they will feel prompted to utter: The Christ-Being. That this is the Christ-Being must be sensed and experienced in an artistic way, and not merely thought out theoretically or intellectually. The most important thing of all is what the forms express artistically. Furthermore — and not through the intellect, which ought merely to be the ladder by way of which experience is attained — this group is intended to urge people to look at it standing there in the east of our building and be able to say: 'That is myself.' It is not an abstract definition of the human being, since balance can be achieved in an infinite number of ways; it is not the image of a god, since Christians, too, are not supposed to make images of their God. It is something that has evolved out of the human group soul and become the force of individuality in every single human being. These forms do justice to the working and weaving of the impulse to individuality.

If you can think about what I have just said without using your intellect, but purely filling it with feeling, and if you can realize that nothing is stated by means of symbols or is intellectually thought out, and that at least the endeavour has been, above all, to let what is expressed stream out into artistic forms, then you will have understood the fundamental principle that this building of the Goetheanum is intended to express. And you will also have understood the way in which the inner spirit of human evolution is connected with the spirit of Anthroposophy. It is not possible today to come close to this spiritual science arising out of Anthroposophy by any other path than the one which leads from the immense demands coming out of this new time of the present and the near future. We really do have to learn to speak in a different way about what it is that is carrying human beings towards the future.

There exist today a good many rather smug secret societies which are actually no more than the bearers of something that is still reaching out from the time before the great turning-point in the fifteenth century; and this often shows, even quite superficially. We have also pointed out a good many times that such things reach into our circles as well.

It happens very often that the special value of some so-called occult stream is attributed to the fact that it is very 'old'. Some go back to the Rosicrucians in the way they do things, but others go back much further, particularly to ancient Egypt. Most people are easily taken in by the mere mention that something about ancient Egyptian temple wisdom is going to be divulged.

As many of our friends already know, we have always stressed that our spiritual movement founded on Anthroposophy has nothing to do with all this harking back to ancient times. Our movement is concerned with what is now, in the present, being revealed directly out of the spiritual world for this physical world. Therefore it has to speak about many things in a manner that differs from that adopted by secret societies — even those deserving to be taken seriously — which base what they have to say on antiquity, yet which still play a large part in the events of human history today. When people who are initiated into certain secrets of present-day secret societies open their mouths to speak, you will hear them talk mainly about three things.

Firstly, they will describe the experience of the genuine seeker after the spiritual world. As soon as he has stepped across the threshold into the spiritual world, he cannot help but encounter powers who are the true enemies of mankind — the true, actually existing opponents of physical human beings living here on earth in the way intended by the divine powers. These people know that whatever is hidden from ordinary human consciousness is interwoven by those powers who — justifiably, to some extent — may be named as the real causes of illness and death, but who are also equally bound up with everything connected with human birth. And you can hear these people say that silence ought to be maintained about these things, because one cannot reveal to ordinary human beings what lies beyond normal consciousness. By ordinary human beings they mean the immature souls who have not yet made themselves strong enough, but of course this is the case with most of mankind.

The second experience is that much of our knowledge based merely on what we observe through our senses is an illusion, a deception; the more exactly something has been researched, the more deceptive it is. Human beings today need a solid foundation on which they can stand; they need to be able to say: This is a fact, because I have seen that it is so. But once they have crossed over the threshold this solid foundation ceases to exist.

The third thing is that when we work with tools or till the soil, or do any other kind of human work, but especially when we weave something into the fabric of the social order, then we are doing something that does not concern human beings alone, but belongs to the whole universe. When a steam engine is built, or when a telephone or a lightning conductor or a table is constructed, or if a sick person is healed, people assume as a matter of course that these are things which take place merely within human evolution on the earth. But this is not the case. In my mystery drama *The Portal of Initiation* I have shown in the scene between Strader and Capesius[1] how events take place in the whole of the universe when something happens here on earth. This is a profound truth.

These are the three experiences preserved within the secret societies in a form appropriate to the middle of the fifteenth century, a form now misunderstood to a high degree. But in future all such things must be spoken about in a different way. I want to give you an idea of how these things must be spoken about in the future, and of how something coming from the secret sources of our striving for knowledge must then flow out into external knowledge of nature and of the social question, and so on.

This immense metamorphosis has to be understood today, because human beings must fully awaken out of their group consciousness into an individual consciousness. So I still want to speak to you about this immense — this historical — metamorphosis.

LECTURE THREE

Dornach, 14 December 1919

You will already have gathered that the spiritual science with which we are concerned is a profound and most earnest requirement of human evolution in our time and in the nearer future. The science of initiation — the science that brings its knowledge over from the other side of the threshold to the spiritual world — is urgently needed for the further evolution of mankind. But all those powers who represent what is 'old' are opposed to anything that can promote a true knowledge of the spiritual world, so the opposition of people in whom the power of what is 'old' is living, must be overcome. The need to re-learn and re-think everything connected with the most important aspects of human evolution must be understood profoundly and seriously. I therefore beg you to support our endeavours to overcome all the sectarian pettiness that still lives, even in anthroposophical souls, and to see the importance of the spiritual science of Anthroposophy for mankind and the world.

Natural science with its great successes — the materialistic concept of universal laws, and the accompanying erroneous social ideas that are so prevalent today — has lulled humanity to sleep, and it still continues to work very powerfully. Any further healthy progress will not be possible unless mankind can be shaken awake. We must not forget that the knowledge of the spirit has powerful enemies in all those who, above all, want what they are used to thinking to continue, simply because they are too lazy to change. It is no good assuming that we can simply ignore the enmity and opposition that increasingly rise up, the more spiritual science becomes known. This is not the right thing to do; just as one does not allow oneself to become infested with vermin but endeavours to rid oneself of them, quite energetically if necessary. Obviously, each case has to be assessed on its merits.

Unfortunately there are still far too few who really understand the seriousness of what is at stake. There are, on the one hand, those who do not want to depart from long-established habits, not for any spiritual reasons but because they are too lazy. On the other hand, the need is great for those who can oppose with all their might the things that are now ripe for decline. We must not let ourselves be held back by having to be considerate towards what is now ripe for decline. People have had ample opportunity to learn how things that are old are continuing in a meaningless way. What we must now kindle in ourselves is enthusiasm for all the new things that are to be incorporated into human evolution.

I recently spoke to you about the tenor of a rather stupid pamphlet written by a certain professor.[1] The same professor has now appeared in Reutlingen near Stuttgart in order to thunder on once again with equally stupid arguments against Anthroposophy. On this occasion our friend, Dr Walter Stein,[2] stood up and argued against him with all the verve necessary today when the full measure of what is at stake is properly understood; and he wrote to his wife and told her about this discussion, which took place a few days ago:

> Yesterday I heard Professor Traub speak in Reutlingen against Steiner. I joined in the discussion. It was a battle for life or death. I exposed Traub as a man without a conscience who had no knowledge whatsoever of the material about which he was speaking. By the time he came to his final words he could only stammer. He was broken. I cornered the clergyman chairing the meeting so thoroughly, with quotations from the Bible, that with reference to the passage where Christ speaks about reincarnation he said: 'Christ is *mistaken* here.' A clergyman from Reutlingen said this! So then I got up and cried: 'Listen to this, a God who is mistaken!' The audience went wild. They tried to interrupt me at first, and prevent me from speaking. People shouted: 'Keep to the point;' and there was shuffling and stamping. But I spoke quite calmly, pointing at Professor Traub, and said: 'It's on his authority!' I was applauded, and won the argument. That man is finished — and today I'm still half dead.[3]

It was not difficult to foresee that strong hatred would be generated against the spiritual science of Anthroposophy. Anyone could have foreseen it who knew how intimately Anthroposophy is bound up with those powers that must be called upon for the progress of human evolution now and in the near future. Anthroposophy must not be confused with slothfulness, nor with an attitude of mind that seeks to achieve delightful feelings in the soul by means of spiritual ideas and concepts. It is perfectly justifiable that Dr Stein should sense it to be a battle for life or death. We are at the very beginning, and against us rages the battle of the will to destroy. Though the impulse of spiritual science has never led us to take steps to be aggressive ourselves, we must not shrink from whatever is necessary to counter the aggressive element that is increasingly coming towards us from outside. We must not let our courage desert us, and we must not imagine we can make progress by being idle. To bring truth into human evolution will not be a comfortable thing to do, and in certain circumstances we must not be content with tolerance.

Things have come to quite a pass if, when driven into a corner, those whose job it is to represent official Christianity find themselves prepared to state: Christ is mistaken! The clergyman is of course not mistaken! When what he has to say is at odds with what the Bible says, then it is Christ, and not the clergyman, who is mistaken! This attitude of mind is widespread today — only we try not to notice it because it is uncomfortable to do so. If we only wanted to, we could notice it everywhere.

To those, though, who can discern the connections in life, it is perfectly clear that the misfortunes of Europe in recent years — however external their manifestations appear to be — are intimately bound up with the habits of thought acquired by human beings, habits which lead them to say gleefully: See what wonderful progress we have made!

Inner objectivity is what is really needed. But under the influence of recent civilization objectivity has been lost. Everywhere, people's personal opinion is what counts. Yet when the history of the last five or six years comes to be written, it will only be possible to do so on the basis of spiritual science. I need only remind you of what has come to be called the outbreak of the world war. In fact what took place was neither an outbreak nor was it a world war, for it was something quite different, which has as yet by no means come to an end. Of the thirty or forty individuals involved, a great many were not fully awake. They did not have full control of all their faculties of soul and spirit; and the dimming of consciousness opens gates which give easy access for ahrimanic powers to influence human decisions and human intentions. Thus ahrimanic powers played a major part in the initial stages of the events that took place in 1914. If only people today wanted to, they could — simply by following events quite externally — discern how necessary it is to bring spiritual knowledge to bear on human evolution. But their habits of thought and habits of feeling and experience keep them far removed from looking at these things with due seriousness.

The time is ripe for human beings who possess the requisite capacities of soul to come to the fore and meet the spiritual impulses that have begun to break in on our physical world since the last third of the nineteenth century. Despite the way in which mankind has embarked on materialism, the gates between the spiritual world and our world have been open since the last third of the nineteenth century. Certainly, the number of people into whose consciousness the spiritual world can already enter is still small. But up to the middle of this century more and more people will have learnt how to harken with delicate intimacy to their inner being, so that with this inner being they can then meet the impulses that want to enter from the spiritual world.

Those who are aware of the truths and the knowledge that must be brought into human evolution know that if the initiation knowledge they hold is not used to inspire natural science, and especially art, then mankind will face a rapid decline, a terrible decline. If the teaching at our universities goes on as it does now for another thirty years, and if people continue to think about social matters in the same way for another thirty years, then, by the middle of this century, Europe will be a desert. However many ideals are set up in one realm or another, however much people talk until they are blue in the face about individual demands made by one group or another, however strongly people imagine that something can be done for the future of mankind so long as they make their demands vociferously enough — everything will be in vain if there is not a fundamental transformation in human souls in the way they think about the relationship between this world and the spiritual world. If nothing is learnt anew in this sense, if people do not reshape their thinking, then a moral deluge will engulf Europe!

People who have knowledge about the other side of the threshold are forced to look on while the confusion, the materialistic tendencies, the social errors continue, because mankind refuses to re-think and re-learn and so slides downhill, purely as a result of laziness in thinking and feeling! We ought to be under no illusion as to the tremendous incentive there is for this situation to come about in what is termed the civilized world. It is natural, in fact, to expect today's human beings, with their arrogance, to reject everything that comes from initiation science. People are so terribly clever, and so very much inclined to scorn anything that can only be achieved through working on the progress of one's own soul. Mankind imagines that it knows everything without having to learn anything.

Neither the physical nor the social problems of today can be solved unless people's thinking, feeling and will can receive inspiration from the spiritual world. Many people think we are making things up when we speak about initiation science or things like the threshold to the spiritual world. Of course not everyone can cross the threshold today; but surely there is nothing to prevent anyone from seeing the sense of what they are told by those who have been across this threshold. Yet again and again we hear the false argument: How can I agree that what so-and-so says about initiation science is right if I can't look into the spiritual world myself? This argument is false. Sound common sense can quite well decide whether what someone is saying is in the line of truth. When a person is speaking about the spiritual world you merely have to observe the manner in which he does so, the seriousness with which he interprets things, the logic of his argument, and so on, and then you can quite well form a judgement about whether what he is saying about the spiritual world is the talk of a charlatan or has a basis in fact. Anyone can form such a judgement, and no one is prevented from bringing inspiration to the realms of nature and society on the basis of what is said by another person who has the right to speak about the principle of initiation.

The forces of human evolution that have been guiding human beings in their progress will be exhausted by the middle of this century, approximately speaking. New forces must be drawn up from the depths of human souls, and people will have to understand how they are linked in the depths of their souls with the roots of spiritual life.

Not everyone can cross the threshold today, because over the course of the last few hundred years human beings have become accustomed to regard everything that comes towards them as taking place in time. The first thing we experience when we cross the threshold, however, is that beyond it there is a world in which time as we know it has no meaning. That is why it is so useful to prepare by making a beginning through thinking backwards about something. Think, for example, about a play with five acts, but begin with the fifth and work your way to the first. Or consider a melody, not in the sequence in which it is composed, but think and feel the notes backwards. Or imagine your day not from morning to evening, but by beginning at the evening and proceeding backwards until you come to the morning. In this way we can seriously train our thinking to suspend time.

In order to think and feel backwards, we have to exert an inner compulsion, and this compulsion is good because it propels us out of the ordinary sense-perceptible world. If we go backwards in our thoughts from evening to morning we are thinking against the flow of time. We suspend time. If we can develop this kind of thinking to the extent that, as far as possible, we can think back into our lives, then we have achieved a great deal. If we cannot extricate ourselves from time we cannot enter into the spiritual world.

We have often said that the human being is composed of a physical body, an etheric body, an astral body, and an ego. The physical and etheric bodies are the only ones that can be considered in connection with the physical, sense-perceptible world. The etheric body still has earthly processes that take place in time, but the astral body can only be found once we have extricated ourselves from time. The physical body exists in space, but the ego, the true ego, can only be found once we have extricated ourselves from space. The world of the true ego is devoid of space.

So amongst our experiences, when we step across the threshold to the spiritual world, is the twofold experience of becoming extricated from time and from space. Consider how much of what you look upon as the content of your consciousness will be lost once you are outside space and time. Your life, even your soul life, is entirely adapted to space and time. But then you enter a world to which you are not adapted, and not being adapted brings with it sensations of pain and suffering. So there is at first no way of entering the spiritual world without overcoming pain and suffering. Although they are not conscious of it, people shy away from the spiritual world out of fear, because they do not want to step into a world that is an abyss of spacelessness and timelessness.

Now that I have opened your spiritual eyes to this first experience on the other side of the threshold, you will have a vivid understanding of why it is that only a few people have, as yet, sufficient inner strength and courage to enter a bottomless, timeless experience. Through their destiny certain people are bound to cross over the threshold. Without the wisdom they can bring back with them it will not be possible for there to be progress. It will be necessary to trust them, and for this the faculty of trust will have to become a fundamental social virtue.

For the education of mankind in general to proceed in a way that will enable human beings to grow into the spiritual world, it will be necessary for people to trust those who have a right to speak about initiation science. They must be met with trust founded not on a blind belief in authority but on sound common sense. Sound common sense, properly applied, will not fail to understand the knowledge brought from the other side of the threshold. Though not everybody is quite so crass as to say: Christ is mistaken — nevertheless this is the way people speak; it is the logic of life today. And when people say that they cannot distinguish between what they are told with inner logic from out of the spiritual worlds and what the professors in the universities tell them, it is because they lack the will to apply any sound common sense. Surely it is possible, out of sound common sense, to say that there is no point in having anything more to do with someone who says: Christ is mistaken.

We have lost any genuine knowledge of the soul. Such a science exists no longer. And the science of the spirit became uncomfortable for the Catholic church as early as the ninth century, when the spirit was abolished at the 8th General Ecumenical Council, the fourth Council of Constantinople in AD 869.[4] This established the dogma that the human being should not think he consisted of body, soul and spirit, but of body and soul only, with the soul possessing some spiritual aspects. Nowadays this is still taught by psychology. People think this teaching is based on objective science, but in fact it is merely a repetition of the dogma of 869.

Everything, too, to do with the soul, was monopolized by the churches in the form of beliefs, creeds and dogmas — everything that people really ought to recognize quite naturally about the soul. The only knowledge that was left free was knowledge about external nature. No wonder, then, that we have no science of the soul nowadays. Worldly scholarship has devoted itself solely to the science of nature, while the science of the soul has been monopolized, and the science of the spirit abolished. If we base our efforts on modern psychology, which is all words — more or less — we shall be unable to come to a real understanding of what is at work in the soul.

You know from my description in *Knowledge of the Higher Worlds* that thinking, feeling and will fall apart in our consciousness when we step across the threshold to the spiritual world. In today's ordinary, everyday consciousness thinking, feeling and will form a kind of chaos; they are both layered and intermingled. But the moment we begin to gain some experience of initiation science, thinking, feeling and will become independent forces within our consciousness. And then we get to know them; then we learn how to distinguish thinking from feeling and from will.

Looking at thinking — not from the point of view of its content but in its aspect as a power within us — we find that this power of thinking is a shining-in of what we experienced in the spiritual worlds before birth, or before conception. The will-nature of man, on the other hand, is something embryonic, something germinating, that will only be fully developed after death. Within the course of a life, thinking — in the way it lives in the person — is merely a semblance, for its true nature lies before birth, or before conception. And the will is something that is merely germinating, and what is to develop from this can only come into being after death. Thinking and will in the human being are fundamentally different.

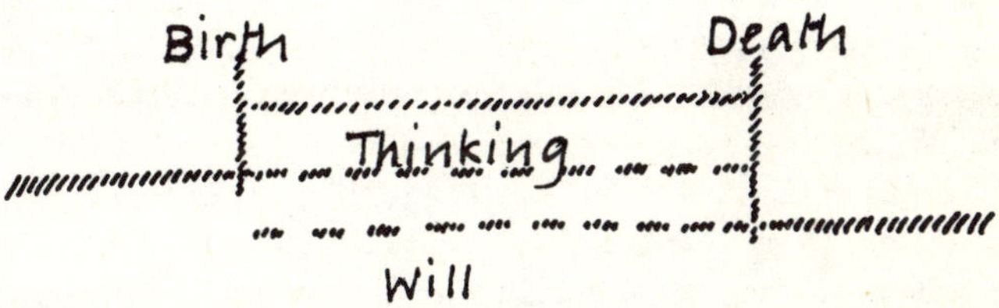

Thus thinking and will are defined, neatly parcelled up and separated out by definition. But definitions lead nowhere, although their shortcomings are usually overlooked. The definition once made in ancient Greece of a human being as a two-legged creature with no feathers is a case in point, since it could equally well describe a plucked chicken.[5] Things are not sufficiently simple to be dealt with by our ordinary intellectual faculties. It is easy enough to state: What we experience as thinking must be said to have its true existence before birth, while what plays into us now is merely like a mirror-image of thinking. But there is a difficulty here, which we can overcome by exerting our thinking just a little.

If we place a mirror on one side, and on the other an object, a candle perhaps, then there will be a mirror-image. You know which is the image and which is the object and are not likely to confuse the two. If you hide the candle behind a screen, then you will see only the image, which will do whatever the candle is doing. And since you are accustomed to thinking in terms of space you can quite easily imagine how the image is related to the reality of the candle. Similarly, our power of thinking is like a mirror-image, and the reality lies before birth. The actual power, of which we use the image in this life, lies before birth. So the principle of human consciousness that arises when we look at our own consciousness is: I think, therefore I am *not*. *Cogito ergo* non *sum*! The principle we have to grasp is that what works in thinking is something like an image, and that the power of thinking lies before birth. Modern progress began when the opposite was posited as a fundamental principle of philosophy: *Cogito ergo sum*, which is a nonsense. As you can see, modern mankind has an exacting test to go through, and we have arrived at a parting of the ways. We must learn to re-think what we consider to be the foundations of soul life.

In the will between birth and death, and what it becomes after death, there is a germination and a fruition. This arrangement of having the image of thinking and the embryo of will is the only thing that makes it possible for us to have freedom between birth and death. You can read about this in my books *The Riddle of Man* and *Von Seelenrätseln*,[6] and also in *The Philosophy of Spiritual Activity*, where these things are dealt with philosophically.

But now we come to the remarkable thing that will show you how unsuited our comfortable everyday thinking is for a comprehension of reality. Having comprehended the nature of thinking, we have to say at the same time: This thinking is not exclusively thinking; it also contains a power of will. The inner being with which we think, we also use for our will. The major part of it is thinking, but it has an undertone of will; and similarly our will has an undertone of thinking.

When you look at reality you do not arrive at concepts which can be fitted into systems, for one thing is always at the same time and in a certain way the other thing. The human being is linked to worlds that are outside the one we see with our eyes and hear with our ears — worlds, however, within which we exist no less than we do in this world of the senses. We cannot say that worlds other than that of the senses are no concern of ours, for we exist in the midst of them. When we walk about here on the earth, when we cleave our way through the air which our senses perceive, we are at the same time cleaving our way through the worlds of the spirit.

We are linked to a certain kind of spiritual existence by what is mainly thinking, with only an undertone of will. And we are linked to another aspect of the spiritual worlds by what is mainly will with less thinking. The profound consequence is that all this expresses itself in human life. The variety in the world has come about because either the one or the other has always been perfected more in one direction or more in another. The forces, for example, that lie in the will, with its undertone of thinking, were most outstandingly perfected in the ancient Hebrew culture. And those forces of the human soul that are founded chiefly in thinking, with its undertone of will, were developed in what we call the ancient pagan culture. In the civilized world these two streams are running alongside and in and out of one another. Our way of looking at the natural, physical world is a continuation of the ancient pagan culture, and in our social views, our ethical attitudes, our religious concepts, we have a continuation of the ancient Hebrew culture.

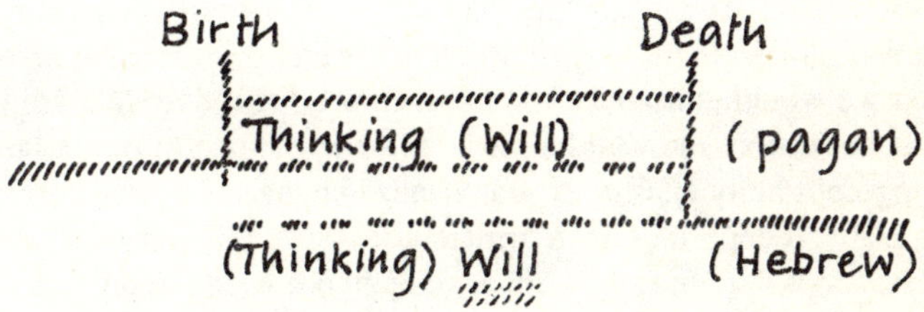

This dualism also lives in every individual human being. A person worships nature in a pagan way on the one hand. And on the other hand, without having found a proper basis in the physical world — apart from taking the habits of thought acquired here over into social science — he ponders deeply about social and even ethical life, coming to the conclusion that there is freedom on the one hand and physical necessity on the other. He enters a ghostly twilight between freedom and necessity in which there seems to be no bridge between the two, and so on; the confusion is immense.

This confusion is in many ways the content of life today as it goes downhill, for there is something lacking. We have our view of the physical world, which is nothing but a continuation of ancient pagan culture. And we have our moral, social views, which are merely a continuation of the Old Testament. Christianity is an episode that was initially comprehended historically but which can now be considered to have slipped through the net of civilization. It is, basically, simply not there. When you listen to people who often speak about Christ you can do what I suggested in connection with Harnack's *What is Christianity?*[7] You can substitute 'God the Father' wherever he writes about 'Christ' — or you can simply put 'god' in the pantheistic sense — and you will find, on the whole, that what he is saying is still the same. Where it is not the same, he is talking nonsense anyway.

All these things have to be said today, because we have to find a foundation for what must be the content of consciousness in the future. In a similar way, you see, the theory of evolution talks about the human being having evolved from lower forms of life, or about these lower forms of life having evolved up to the level of the human being. Indeed, you will find in my *Occult Science* that from a particular point of view we have to agree with this.

The human head that we carry on our shoulders today is already in the process of evolving downwards again. If the rest of our organism were organized in the way in which our head is organized at present, then we would constantly be in the process of dying. We are only alive because of the vital forces working in the rest of our organism being constantly sent up to our head. Our head is a creature permanently dying; it is in regression. But for this very reason the elements of soul and spirit can develop in our head. And in our head lies the undertone of will that is a part of our thinking. This undertone of will is what provides the constant impetus towards dying, towards an overcoming of physical matter.

When we then actually die, the will comes into play. When our body is given over to the earth, then what has been going on in our head from birth until death continues, quite physically, in the earth's body. When you die, what you do between birth and death inside your skin continues outside, in the earth. Because bodies are laid into the earth, the earth thinks in accordance with the very principle which you apply when you think with your human head. By going through the gate of death we carry into the physical earth, with our decomposing or cremated body, that process which we otherwise take for ourselves during life between birth and death.

This is a fact of natural science, and people in the future must know these facts. With regard to these things natural science is at present no more than child's play, since it cannot get around to thinking about them and conducting research into them.

Conversely, the destructiveness that has developed in our head is the continuation of what existed before conception. The destruction only begins at birth, since that is when we acquire our head. Prior to that it was not destruction. With this we are touching upon an extremely important mystery of world existence. What lives in our head, what has taken place in the spiritual worlds before we enter our physical body, continues as a force within our head, making it possible for us to enter into relationships with other people and with the physical world. If we can understand this thoroughly, we shall be able to see how forces from the spiritual worlds play into this physical world.

A concrete example will best show what is meant (the years are written on the blackboard). Goethe died in 1832, and very little of the force of his spirit played into the period up to 1865, the first generation after his death. Not until 33 years had gone by would something coming from him into our earthly evolution begin to be noticeable. And this grew stronger and stronger until 1898. After a further 33 years we come to 1931, which would be the second period when Goethe's forces were at work. And in 1964 the third period would end. An example like this teaches us that relatively soon after a person has passed through the gate of death the forces he then unfolds begin to play into what goes on here on earth. But you have to know how this happens. Those who do spiritual work, who really work with their spirit, know how forces from the spiritual world are active within the forces they are using for their work.

My statement that the middle of the present century will be an important point in time is based on just such observations as those depicted in this example. Observations like this teach us how the forces of the spiritual world play into the physical world. This middle point of our century coincides with the end of the period in which the forces from before the middle of the fifteenth century — still atavistically with us to some extent — reach their ultimate decadence. By the middle of our present century mankind must have taken the decision to turn towards the spirit. Yet there are still people who ask why the catastrophe will come and why the gods will not help. The answer is, quite simply, that we are living in a period of human evolution when the gods are only too ready to help, if human beings will come forward to meet them. But they have to work in accordance with their own laws, which stipulate that they must work with free human beings, and not with puppets.

Until the middle of the fifteenth century, a person with spiritual knowledge, speaking about the phenomena of human birth and death, would have shown how destiny between birth and death was woven out of the divine world. But today we have to point out that a person's destiny is determined by his previous lives on earth, and by the manner in which these lives cause him to create the forces that will enable the divine worlds to come towards him. Today we have to seek in the human being himself the source out of which the forces arise which enable spiritual beings of one kind or another to approach him. This is the important point we have now reached in earthly evolution. What is happening externally must be seen as an expression of inner events which can only be understood through the insights of spiritual science.

It is possible for every single human being today to observe the distant estuary of the river of events. Enough people have been murdered over the last four or five years — ten or twelve million at least, in the civilized world, or probably more — and three times as many have been crippled in the various countries. Such is the marvellous progress our civilization has made! But this will gradually have to be recognized as the distant estuary of the river of events, while the source of that river will have to be sought in what takes place in human souls when they brace themselves against the spiritual world that wants to break in and carry the human being into the future. All things must now be seen from this point of view, with greater and greater insight.

But I now want to conclude quite bluntly with something of immediate interest — since the particular slant of these three lectures has arisen out of the presence of a number of friends from England; something which has given us great pleasure: It is possible today to speak of the victors and the vanquished. This is an obvious point of view, but there is another that could be much more important. It is possible to ask: What is it that has changed in the so-called vanquished, and what has changed in the so-called victors?

Well, the actual victor is the being of the Anglo-American peoples, and, as a result of forces that I have often described here,[8] this being of the Anglo-American peoples is destined to dominate the world in the future. So what is the consequence for the German nation of being eliminated from experiencing the things that will in future dominate the external world? The responsibility of the nation as a whole — though not, of course, that of individuals — for the events of human evolution falls away. The responsibility — not of the individual, but of the nation — is lifted from those who are downtrodden, as indeed they are. They will not be able to recover, and any talk in that vein is founded on short-sightedness. They are relieved of responsibility.

All the greater, though, will be the responsibility on the other side, where the real responsibility will lie. It will be easy to win external dominion, for this will be done with the help of forces for which the winners can claim no credit. The transfer of external dominion will take place with the relentlessness of a force of nature. The resulting responsibility, however, will be deeply significant for those souls. Already inscribed in the book of human destiny is the question: Will there be a sufficient number among those impelled to assume external dominion, as though by a force from outside, who feel a responsibility for inserting into this entirely external, materialistic dominion — for that is what it will be, make no mistake — an impetus for spiritual life?

What is more, there is not much time in which this can be done. The middle of this century is a very important moment. Those who have been chosen to shoulder the dominion of materialism in the external world must feel the full weight of this responsibility. For the dominion of materialism bears within it the seed of destruction. To shoulder external dominion means to take on, and to live within, the forces of destruction, the forces of sickness in mankind. Out of the new seed of the spirit will come something that can bear mankind onwards into the future. This seed will have to be nurtured, and those to whom dominion has fallen will be especially responsible for this.

Serious and thorough-going thought must be given to these things, thought that is not merely seemingly spiritual, while in actual fact being materialistic. Two points are frequently made. On the one hand there is the cheap objection: What is the point in going on about social ideas; bread doesn't grow out of social ideas. And on the other hand it is said: Once people find work again, everything will be better and the social question will look quite different. Both of these are materialism in disguise, for both lead to a denial of spiritual life.

In the first place, what is the difference between human beings and animals? Animals go and find their food by instinct, and if there isn't enough they starve. Human beings work to create food, and once they begin to work they begin to have thoughts. Only when thoughts begin does the social question arise. If human beings are to work, they must have a stimulus to work, but the stimulus that has existed hitherto will cease to be there in the future. There will have to be a new stimulus for work. What has to be said is that once people give out thoughts that come from a feeling of responsibility for the world, thoughts that will carry their souls, then the forces that emerge from these thoughts will go over into hand and will, and work will arise. Everything depends on the thoughts. And the thoughts depend on whether we open our hearts to the impulses of the spiritual world.

LECTURE FOUR

Dornach, 15 December 1919

The tasks facing mankind now and in the near future are decisive, far-reaching and important, and to take part in mastering them will require powerful courage of soul. Looking at them in depth and endeavouring to reach an understanding of what is really needed today can prompt us to question the easy superficiality with which so-called public matters are taken in hand nowadays, when politics appear quite random and haphazard. People form their opinions about life on the basis of a few emotional reactions to views that are entirely personal, or merely concern their own nation. Yet the seriousness of our present predicament would be better met by a desire to gain a proper foundation on which to base a truly sound judgement. I have spoken a great deal here about the demands of contemporary events,[1] always with the aim of enabling people to form their own opinion, and not to present them with ready-made views. The most important thing today is to want to find out the facts of life with ever-increasing thoroughness, in order to acquire a foundation on which to base a judgement.

Far too few questions are asked concerning the really grave, actual facts. People who consider themselves to be most eminently practical are, actually, the greatest theoreticians, because they are content with merely forming a few ideas about life on which to base their opinions. Yet only a thoroughgoing and all-embracing enquiry into life itself can provide a basis for a practical assessment of what is really needed. To make politics at random or create wonderful theories about life without any foundation in reality is, to say the least, intellectually frivolous, and our hope must be that people will develop an inner seriousness about life.

What we might call the practical side of our spiritual science has most recently been offered to the world in the threefold ordering of the social organism.[2] Yet the very way in which we have to think and form ideas in order to work out this threefold ordering is met with prejudice both in thought and in feeling. People have ideas about what the truth is, about what is good, what is right and what is practical and so on. Having formed them, they assume that these ideas must have absolute validity everywhere and for every age. A socialist in western or central or eastern Europe is likely to have certain quite specific socialist ideals, founded on the fundamental belief that because they satisfy him they will also satisfy all other human beings anywhere on the earth, and that they will remain eternally valid for the whole of the earth's future.

Since people fail to understand that ideals for social life have to be born out of the fundamental tenor of an age and of a place, they do not easily realize how necessary it is to introduce the threefold ordering of the social organism with varying nuances to Europe, as well as to its outpost, America. Once it is introduced, the necessary nuances will come about quite naturally in relation to the different peoples. The ideas are not absolute; they are for our present time and for the near future. But in order to assess the full importance of separating out within the social organism an independent cultural life, an independent life of rights and the state, and an independent economic life, we must look open-mindedly at the way in which culture, state and economy came to be mingled together in our European-American civilization. The origin of our cultural life is entirely different from that of the life of rights and the state, and quite different again from that of our economic life. These three strands of such differing origin are chaotically entangled. Today I want to go right back to the source of these three strands. (See drawing, p. 45)

A realistic, quite external, assessment will find that we assimilate our culture by allowing the continuation of the culture of ancient Greece and ancient Rome to work on us. Graeco-Latin culture flowed into what later became our grammar schools and universities. Education in the humanities, even right down into primary schools, stems from the Greek element (orange in the drawing). Our European cultural life goes back to ancient Greece, for Roman culture was merely a transitional stage. Of course, in more recent times this Greek culture has become intermingled with mechanical technology, commercial technology, and so on; to our universities have been added technical colleges, commercial colleges and others which add a more modern element. These things do not only enter the souls of some so-called educated class, for the socialist theories of today that have taken hold of proletarian thought are also merely an adaptation of something stemming from Greek cultural life which has been through a series of metamorphoses.

This Greek cultural life — what we find in Plato, in Heraclitus, in Pythagoras, in Empedocles, and especially in Anaxagoras — all goes back to oriental culture. But it underwent a significant transformation on its way from the Orient to Greece. In the Orient this culture was far more spiritual, and it flowed from what we could call the Mysteries of Spirit, or I could say the Mysteries of Light (drawing continues). Greek culture was filtered and diluted in comparison with the oriental culture and spiritual life from which it originated.

We have to go back into prehistoric times because the Mysteries of Light, or of Spirit, belong to pre-history. Right back in the third, fourth, fifth, sixth, even seventh millennium before the Mystery of Golgotha, there were human beings throughout the civilized Asiatic world for whom spiritual truths were revealed through their natural clairvoyance, which was bound up with the blood and with the organization of the physical body. I am speaking of the widespread population of the whole region.

But their atavistic clairvoyance was growing increasingly decadent, and this was not merely a cultural phenomenon but also one affecting people's social life. This was because, out of the widespread mass of the earth's population, there appeared from various centres — but chiefly from one particular centre in Asia — a type of human being with special capacities. These people still had their atavistic clairvoyance; a dreamy consciousness of the secrets of the universe still arose out of their inner soul life. And in addition, they had what we call the power of thought. They were the first human beings in whom intelligence began to dawn.

This was a very telling social phenomenon. Those ancient people — who had nothing but dreamy visions about the secrets of the universe — saw immigrants entering into their territory whom they could certainly understand, for they also had the same visions. But these immigrants also had something which they lacked — this was the power of thought. When they moved southwards from the higher northern regions of Asia, they came to be known as Aryans.

The Mysteries of Spirit, or specifically the Mysteries of Light, were founded by people who combined atavistic clairvoyance with the first flaring up of intelligence — the inner spark of the human being — a final outcome of which is our present cultural life. Much of what was then revealed has been preserved within mankind. But we must not forget that as early as ancient Greek times the more cultured people witnessed the extinguishing of the old gift of atavistic clairvoyance. By Roman times, the only thing left was the power of thought, whereas the Greeks still had an awareness of the fact that the power of thought came from the same source as the old, atavistic clairvoyance. That is why Socrates still experienced something that he called his *daimon*,[3] even though this only inspired him with dialectic truths of the intellect.

The ancient Greeks have also shown very tellingly in their art how the human bearer of intelligence stands out from the rest of humanity. A thorough study of Greek sculpture will reveal three strongly differentiated types. The Aryan type is shown in the head of Apollo, Pallas-Athene, Zeus or Hera. Compare the ears of an Apollo with those of a Mercury and you will see how the types differ. In the Mercury type the Greeks wanted to show how what merged with the intelligence was the ancient, bygone clairvoyance that still lived on as superstition, and how it was a lower form of culture lying at the foundation of civilization. At the very bottom of society stood the races who still possessed the remnants of the ancient clairvoyance and who lived in the peripheral regions of Greece and were recorded in the satyr type. Compare a satyr nose with a Mercury nose, or satyr ears with Mercury ears. The Greeks showed in their art what they carried in their consciousness about their evolution.

What came through the Mysteries of Spirit or of Light, and was gradually filtered through ancient Greece until it arrived in modern times, was also able to create the basis for the life of rights. On the one hand there is the revelation of the gods in the Mysteries that bring the spirit to human beings, and on the other there is the planting of this spirit derived from the gods into the external social organism, into the theocracies. And the theocracies were capable not only of disseminating the life of rights, the political life, out of the Mysteries, but they were also able to regulate the economic life out of this spirit. The priests of the Mysteries of Light were at the same time the economic and commercial administrators of their regions. They built houses and canals and bridges, and they saw to the cultivation of the soil, and so on.

The whole of this civilization was thus originally founded on the cultural life, but gradually it became abstract, nothing but a collection of ideas. By the Middle Ages it had become theology, which is a compilation of concepts that replaced the old cultural, spiritual life. Because the connection with the spirit had been lost, things had to be run in an abstract way by a *curia*. The western ruler has nothing to show for the fact that he is descended from the theocratic ruler, who received his mandate through the Mysteries from the gods. All he has left are his crown and his coronation robe, his outer insignia. Now everything has become externalized.

Hardly less externalized are the teachings that flow through our grammar schools and universities. They are the ultimate echo of the messages received from the gods in the Mysteries. Spiritual, cultural life has become totally abstract. It has become what in the final analysis is now talked about in socialist circles: an ideology, a collection of thoughts that are nothing but thoughts.

Today's social chaos has evolved because a cultural life that is so filtered, so abstract, loses all its impetus. It is now up to us to place cultural life on its own foundation once more, so that it can flourish again. We must find the way from spirit that is nothing but a thought, back to the creative spirit. An independent cultural life will be strong enough to come alive again. A spiritual, cultural life held in check by the leading-strings of the church, or preserved and protected by the state, or staggering under the burden of commerce and economy, cannot become fruitful for mankind. Only a free and independent spiritual life of culture can do so.

It is now high time for us to engender courage in our souls with which to stand up before the world, and frankly to point out that cultural, spiritual life must be put back on to its own foundations. Many people are now asking what they can do. The first thing to do is to help as many people as possible to understand how necessary it is, for example, that cultural life should stand on its own foundations, to understand that the education of the nineteenth century in primary and secondary schools and universities is no longer of any use for mankind, and that a new education must be built out of an independent spiritual life of culture. There is as yet little courage in people's souls with which to stand up and make these demands for radical change. And such demands can only be made once enough work has been done to give as many people as possible the necessary insight into the situation. Any other kind of social work undertaken today is merely provisional. Creating insight into these things with every means at our disposal is what we ought to be doing today. We must become productive by making the cultural life of the spirit free and independent.

The Mysteries of Light are present in a less filtered degree in today's oriental culture and spiritual life than they are in the West. If we look closely at what the Hindus or the oriental Buddhists have, we are far more likely to discern traces of that from which our own spiritual, cultural life also descends; only in Asia it has remained at a different stage. We, however, are unproductive to a great degree. When news of the Mystery of Golgotha spread westwards, where did the Greek and Latin scholars find the concepts with which to comprehend it? They found them in oriental wisdom. The West did not produce Christianity; it came from the East. Furthermore, at a time when spiritual culture in English-speaking parts of the world was felt to be unfruitful, and when people there were longing for a new inspiration, the theosophists turned to the colonized Indians and sought from them the source of a new Theosophy.[4] There was no fruitful source in their own environment. Besides this significant example, there are many others that prove the barrenness of spiritual life in the West. And every proof is also proof of the need to make spiritual, cultural life independent within the threefold order of the social organism.

A second strand in the tangle is that of the life of the state, of rights and the law. This second strand is the scourge of our civilization. Looking upon it from the outside we see the learned judges on their benches, passing sentence, together with the jury, on crimes and offences. We see officials administering our civilized world with their red tape, to the despair of those who are thus administered. Everything we call jurisprudence or the state, and all the politics that arise out of a combination of jurisprudence and the state, belong to this strand (see drawing, p. 45, white). This (orange) is the strand of spiritual, cultural life. And this (white) is the strand of rights and the state.

Where does it come from? It goes back to the Mystery culture of ancient Egypt, which then passed through parts of southern Europe and through the sober, unimaginative nature of the Romans, where it united with a side branch of oriental culture to culminate in Catholic Christianity, or rather the Catholic church (see drawing). This Catholic church is in itself a kind of jurisprudence. From the separate dogmas right up to that mighty final reckoning known throughout the Middle Ages and beyond as the Last Judgment, the whole — so very different — spiritual life of the Orient was given an Egyptian slant by the Mysteries of Space, so that what transpired was like a society of world judges passing universal sentence and meting out universal punishments: a society of sinners, a society of the good and the bad.

This is the second strand in the tangle we call civilization; it has not united in any organic way with the rest, as you will easily discover if you go to a university and listen to a legal lecture about state law and then, perhaps, a theological lecture about canon law. They go along side by side. These things have moulded human life. Even in these late times when their origins have been forgotten, they still structure the life of human souls. The life of rights later worked to make cultural, spiritual life abstract, and in external life it created social customs, social habits, social institutions.

The final social outcome of the decadent spiritual stream of the East is the feudal aristocracy (see drawing). Because he has divested himself of everything spiritual, there is no way of telling that an aristocrat originated in the oriental, theocratic spiritual life. And then there was something that passed through the Roman church constitution, through theocratizing law, through legislatorial theocracy, and became worldly in the city states of the Middle Ages, and totally worldly in modern times. In its ultimate outcome it is the bourgeoisie (see drawing). Thus all these spiritual forces are well and truly mixed together in their ultimate outcome.

There is also a third strand connected with all this. Seen from the outside (see drawing, red), where is it most characteristic? In the customs of commercial life, whose origins lie in the national habits of the Anglo-American world, we find the ultimate outcome of what I would like to call the Mysteries of Earth, of which the Druid Mysteries were only one particular variety. Those European tribes who were entirely ignorant and barbaric in the face of the revelations of oriental wisdom, in the face of the Mysteries of Space, in the face of everything that later became Catholicism, those European tribes who came to meet Christianity as it was spreading — they had a specific form of wisdom that was totally and utterly physical.

Historically, only the ultimate customs stemming from this remain to be studied, the festivals of those whose customs have become the practices of England and America. These festivals were quite different from those of ancient Egypt, where the harvest was related to the stars. Here (red strand) the harvest itself was the festival. The highest festivals of the year were related to the economic life.

An overall spiritual view shows how human beings bring over from Asia and up from the South a life of culture and a life of rights that they receive from above and bring down to the earth. Here, in this third strand, an economic life springs up that has to evolve upwards. It is an economic life which enveloped the usages of right and the matters of culture to such an extent that, for example, the impregnation of the herds was celebrated as a special festival in honour of the gods. There were other such festivals, all arising out of the economic life. In northern Russia, central Russia, Sweden, Norway, or in territories that until recently were parts of Germany, in northern France, and in the Great Britain of today, we find populations which had a distinct economic civilization long before the spread of Christianity in the olden days. The old customs, customs belonging to the life of rights and the cultural life, all contain echoes of this ancient economic civilization.

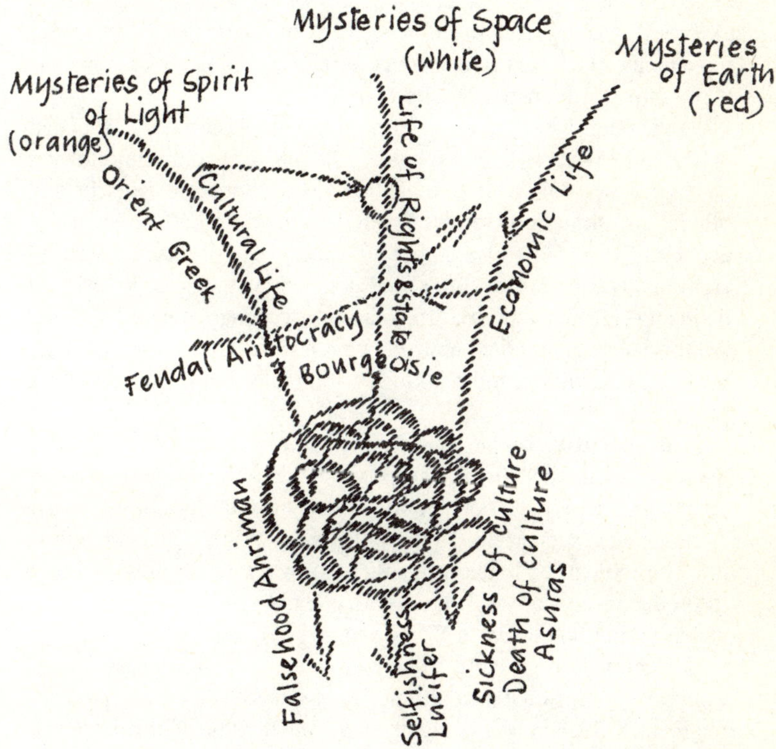

This economic civilization comes face to face with all that enters in from the other sides. Its original usages of right have been discarded because Roman law has flowed in, and its original usages of cultural life have been discarded because the cultural life of Greece has flowed in. At first this economic life is sterile, but gradually it works its way up again; but it can only do so if it can overcome the chaos that arises from the acceptance of a cultural life and a life of rights from outside.

Look at Anglo-American cultural life today, and you will find in it two starkly differing elements. In the first place, more than elsewhere in the world, you have what are called the secret societies, which exercise more influence than people realize. They are proud to be custodians of ancient Egyptian and oriental culture, but this has become so filtered, so diluted, that it now consists of nothing but symbols. And these symbols are no longer understood, even though they exercise a considerable influence among the leaders of these movements. This was an ancient cultural life, and is not one that has come into being on the West's own soil.

On the other hand there is a cultural life that is certainly grounded on the soil of the economic sphere, although so far only tiny flowers have grown from it. Locke, Hume, Mill, Spencer, Darwin and others[5] are these tiny flowers that have grown up out of the soil of economic life. Mill's ideas, Spencer's ideas may be exactly deduced from this economic life. But social democracy has made theories of them and considers cultural life to be an appendage of economic life. All this has been dredged up from what is thought of as practical life but which is, in fact, more a kind of routine of living and not a true practice of life.

Thus we find on the one hand such things as the teachings of Darwin, Spencer, Mill and Hume, and on the other the filtered Mystery teachings that find their continuation in the various sectarian developments such as the Theosophical Society, the Quakers, and so on. The economic life that is trying to grow has so far only managed to produce a few tiny flowers, while the cultural life and the life of rights remain alien plants the further we go westwards.

In Central Europe there has always been a defensiveness, a kind of opposition, against the cultural life of Greece on the one hand and the Roman Catholic life of rights on the other. Philosophy in Central Europe is one example of this rebellion. In England there is virtually no understanding of Central European philosophy. It is, in fact, impossible to translate Hegel into the English language,[6] so nothing is known about him. German philosophy is thought of as something typically German, with which sensible people can have no truck. And yet in German philosophy we have a late flowering of this rebellion, especially in Fichte, Schelling and Hegel. Even earlier, in Goethe, we find the search for an independent cultural, spiritual life. He wanted nothing of the last echoes of Roman Catholic jurisprudence in what had come to be called the laws of nature. In the expression 'the laws of nature' — the 'laws' — you can feel how jurisprudence still has a ghostly presence in natural science. But Goethe's natural science has to do solely with archetypal phenomena, with ultimate facts, in which natural 'laws' have no meaning. It was the first advance towards an independent cultural life.

In Central Europe we also have the first advance towards an independent life of rights. Read Wilhelm von Humboldt's essay *The Sphere and Duties of Government*,[7] and you will see a first attempt at constructing an independent life of rights or of the state, an endeavour to find independence for the political realm. Attempts like this go back to the end of the eighteenth century. It was in Central Europe that these attempts took shape, founded on important impulses which should not be ignored, for they, too, can lead over into the impulse for the threefold ordering of the social organism.

Right at the beginning of my book on Nietzsche[8] I quoted a sentence that gives us a sense of the tragedy of German cultural and spiritual life. In his essay on David Strauss he described the founding of the German Reich in 1870/1 as: 'The extirpation of the German spirit in favour of the German Reich.' Since that event, the throat of the German spirit has indeed been well and truly cut. When, in the last five or six years, three-quarters of the world fell upon what once was Germany, all that in fact remained for them to attack was the corpse of German cultural life. By saying these things I do not intend to give the impression that there is not still a great deal within this German cultural life that will have to be taken into account.

What was it, ultimately, that led to the downfall of the Germans? This is a question that must for once be answered without prejudice. The downfall of the Germans came about because they wanted to join in the conduct of materialism while having, in fact, no talent for materialism. Others have considerable talent for materialism. But the Germans tend to retreat when it would be better for them to step forward courageously, and to rush forward when it would be better for them to exercise restraint.[9] Goethe is a good example of this phenomenon. Although he was capable of developing a spirituality — in such works as *Faust* or *Wilhelm Meister* — which could have revolutionized the world, he was unable to make the step that would have brought him to the beginnings of spiritual science. The external personality of this genius finally became a portly official of the court in Weimar, a tremendously industrious minister, who, in the end, could not avoid making compromises, especially in political life.

People would do well to recognize that the likes of Goethe and Humboldt represent possible beginnings, and that they ignore at their peril what lives in German evolution as a whole, which must be developed. For Germans lack the capacity — found increasingly, the further westwards we go — to ascend to the final abstractions. People call what they find in German culture 'abstract' because they fail to experience it. Having squeezed the life out of their own culture, they imagine that the culture of others is also without life. The Germans, however, lack the ability to press forward to ultimate abstractions. This is revealed above all in their state and its life, this most unfortunate of all state existences.

If the Germans had possessed from the beginning the great talent for monarchy that the French have to this day, they would never have fallen victim to 'Wilhelmism'. There was no need for them to choose, or keep in office, so strange a caricature of a monarch. The French may call themselves republicans, but they still have among them an invisible monarch who holds the state and its structure together and keeps a stranglehold on people's hearts and minds — and that is Louis XIV, whose spirit is still everywhere to be found.[10] It is something that is decadent now, of course, but it is still there.

In another vein, the talent for abstraction that has made its appearance in Woodrow Wilson[11] is the most extreme that can appear in outer political life. The words of those Fourteen Points elaborated by that universal schoolmaster are all stamped with impracticality and unfeasibility. They could only come from a spirit that is constructed exclusively for abstraction and has no sense whatever for reality. There are, perhaps, two things that cultural history in the future will find it hard to comprehend. The one is the Kant-Laplace theory of a universal mist out of which everything around us today is supposed to have become distilled. The second will be the unbelievable fact that once upon a time such vast numbers of people could have taken the humbug of Woodrow Wilson's Fourteen Points so seriously in an age when the social situation was so dire.

When we look at the things going on in the world, one beside the other, we discover that the economic life, the political life of rights, and the cultural life are all entangled. If we do not want to perish under a cultural life and life of rights that are degenerate in the extreme, we have no choice but to organize society in a threefold way. In such a society the economic life will grow out of independent roots. It wants to grow, but it cannot do so unless a life of rights and a life of culture come towards it out of freedom. People today must be shown how the economic life, introduced by Anglo-American habits of thought, is creeping along the ground, and that it will only be able to climb its way upwards if it works in harmony with those things which people in other spheres are capable of doing and for which they have talents. If this does not happen, world dominance by the economic life will be a catastrophe.

If the affairs of the world proceed as they are doing at the moment with the degenerate spiritual, cultural life coming from the Orient, then this spiritual life will rush headlong into the most terrible falsehood. Nietzsche had to describe how even the Greeks were forced to protect themselves against the falsehood of existence by means of their art.[12] In the end, art is the divine child that preserves human beings from sinking down into falsehood. But if this first branch of culture is followed one-sidedly, it becomes a stream that flows into falsehood (see drawing p. 45). Of all the years of world history, the last five or six have been those in which the greatest mendacity has been rife among civilized human beings. Hardly any truth at all has been spoken in public life.

Whereas this strand flows into falsehood (see drawing p. 45), this middle one flows into selfishness. And if the Anglo-American economic life, which ought to flow out into world dominance, does not take the trouble to become filled with an independent cultural, spiritual life and an independent life of rights and the state, it will flow into a third abyss of human existence. The first abyss is that of falsehood, the degeneration of humanity by Ahriman. The second is the abyss of selfishness, the degeneration of humanity by Lucifer. And the third, in the physical realm, is sickness and death, and in the cultural realm the sickness and death of culture.

The Anglo-American element may well achieve world dominion, but without the threefold ordering of society this dominion will flood the world with the death of culture and the sickness of culture. These are a gift of the Asuras,[13] just as falsehood is a gift of Ahriman, and selfishness a gift of Lucifer.

From these facts we must draw enthusiasm with which to seek for ways and means to enlighten as many people as possible. Today's task for those who know about these things is to do this very thing. With what we can gain from the practical aspect of the spiritual science of Anthroposophy we must do whatever is in our power against that stupidity which fancies itself to be wisdom and imagines itself to have achieved such heights.

If I have managed with these words to arouse in you a sense for the deep seriousness with which we have to approach these things, then perhaps I have succeeded in achieving something of what I set out to achieve. I wanted to awaken in you a sense that the most important social work we can do today is to explain these things to as wide a circle of people as possible.

LECTURE FIVE

Dornach, 20 February 1920

Our English friends will soon be returning to their country, and since I want to give them as much as possible to take back with them, today's lecture, and the next two, will be set apart from our current theme.[1] These lectures are intended to give them support in the work awaiting them, and today I want to go into some aspects of the evolution — in the spiritual sense — of imperialism through the ages.

We are now in a period of history that can only be understood if we know where the social environment in which we find ourselves has come from. The imperialism we see functioning today and on into the future is borne by the Anglo-American peoples. It is economic imperialism, and it has only recently come into play. The important point about everything that is said with reference to it is that there is no truth in any of it. It floats in the air and leads more or less consciously to untruthfulness. So in order to see that realities in our time are in fact quite different from what we think, we shall have to delve more deeply.

An example of the public's capacity to make judgements nowadays has been the recent glorification of Woodrow Wilson[2] in various parts of Europe. We are now beginning to hear reports that people in America are thinking of declaring him unfit to govern because they have doubts about his judgement. Another example might be the fact that while, over the last four or five years, a great deal has been said about the self-determination of nations and so on, none of these things was true, because behind them there lurked something quite different: namely, questions of power.

To understand these things we must go back to the realities that lie behind what is said and thought and judged. Take the word 'imperialism' — the 'Imperial Federation' has been an official expression for it in England since the beginning of the twentieth century.[3] To understand what such things mean we have to take into account that they are the latest products of an evolution that can only be explained by a genuine view of history.

Let us go back several thousand years before the beginning of the Christian era, when we shall find empires in Asia and a derivative of such empires in Egypt. The Persian empire, and especially the

Assyrian empire, are typical of this oriental impulse. But we shall fail to understand the impetus behind the Assyrian empire unless we go back to still earlier oriental conditions. Even in China — whose organization harks back to extremely distant, long-gone ages — it is no longer possible to recognize the real character of an oriental empire as it used to exist, though there you can still look back beyond the historically-known conditions and see what they are actually founded on.

We cannot understand the ancient imperialism of the Orient unless we know how the consciousness of the population related to what today we would call the ruler or the rulers. Words such as 'ruler' or 'king' no longer express what used to be felt. Indeed it is now very difficult to have any idea about the feelings prevalent three or four thousand years before the Christian era, because it is very difficult to sense how people in those ancient times conceived of the spiritual world in relation to the physical. Nowadays, if people think about a spiritual world at all, they think of it as being somewhere in a distant 'beyond', whereas essentially in olden times no distinction whatsoever was made between the physical world and the spiritual world.

People today can barely make sense of things said now about those ancient times, for the world of ideas was so utterly different. Things that were physically present — such as rulers, dominant castes, slaves, subjugated peoples — were seen as reality *per se*, they were physical reality and spiritual reality at one and the same time. And the ruler of an oriental empire was the god. There was no god beyond the clouds, no choir of spiritual beings surrounding a god on high, such as people came to imagine later on. What we now call ministers of state, even slavish courtiers perhaps, were then beings of a divine nature. It was obvious to people in those days that the schooling in the Mysteries which these human beings had undergone had made them into something higher than ordinary people. So they looked up to them, just as people in Protestant circles look up to their God, or those in more liberally-minded circles look up to their invisible angels and similar beings. These people of the ancient Orient did not have invisible angels or a supersensible, invisible god who was set apart from them. Everything spiritual lived also in human beings. A human soul lived in an ordinary person, and a divine soul, a god, lived in one whom today we would call a ruler.

Today there is no concrete picture of an existing, actual, divine realm that is at the same time a physical realm. Nowadays it seems absurd to say that a king possesses real divine power and divine dignity, but in ancient oriental empires this was the reality. Nobody there spoke about something being exclusively spiritual.

The most ancient forms of imperialism date from when the king or the ruler is the god, a son of heaven who has appeared physically on the earth, or even a heavenly father. From this was derived the manner in which imperialistic conquests came to be justified, as may still be seen in ancient Assyrian documents. Such conquests were simply carried out, just like that, and the right to embark on them was derived from a bounden duty to expand the divine empire ever further and further. This was not a matter of spreading religious beliefs; there was no need for that, since everything was conceived of as being perfectly real within the physical world itself. Those who had been vanquished gave external recognition and obedience to the conqueror, and that was all. In every other way it was up to them to believe whatever they liked. A belief was one's own personal opinion, it was no one else's business.

This was the first form in which imperialism made its appearance. In the second form, the one who was to take on the ruling, leading role was not himself the god, but he was the one who had been sent by the god, inspired by the god, or filled with the divine. In the first phase of imperialism everything was real. When an oriental ruler of that time appeared before his people he wore his robes because they were the vestments of a god, and this was what a god looked like. And his paladins were not official servants but higher beings who surrounded him and did what they did on the strength of their status as higher beings.

Then came the time when people perceived the ruler and also his paladins as emissaries from the gods, beings filled with the divine; they were representatives. This is still quite obvious in Dionysius the Areopagite.[4] You will find in his descriptions of the hierarchy of deacons, archdeacons, bishops, archbishops — the whole hierarchy of the church — an image of the supersensible God with his archai, archangels and angels. Up above is the heavenly hierarchy and down below is a likeness of it, the worldly hierarchy. The deacons and archdeacons put on their vestments and conduct their services because these things are tokens and symbols — whereas in the first phase everything was reality. To people's ordinary way of thinking today, even among the Catholic population, there is scarcely any awareness of the fact that the deacons, priests, deans, bishops and archbishops are the representatives, the deputies, of the heavenly hierarchies.

As imperialism advanced in this way a kind of schism occurred, a real split. On the one hand what shone through the rulers was their aspect of being emissaries of the gods, or of being priests, where priests are at the same time kings. On the other hand the worldly aspect shone through, even though this still came by the grace of the gods, in that they were authorized or appointed by them. Basically, these are merely two versions which show up later in history, when some towns and cities come to be under the jurisdiction of the Church and others under that of the Empire.

In the empires of the first phase, when everything was a reality in the physical world, such a thing would have been unthinkable. But in the second phase some leaders were more secular, though still appointed by God, while others, more ecclesiastical, were also appointed by God. This continued into the Middle Ages. The widespread Roman Church existed externally, coloured more by the priestly aspect. But something that was kept going all through the Middle Ages and beyond, while strictly retaining here on earth the aspect of being sent by God, was the Holy Roman Empire of the German Nation,[5] which only disappeared in 1806. The word 'Holy' retains a hint of something that used to be divine here on earth in ancient times. The word 'Roman' signifies the place of its origin. And the words 'German Nation' describe the more worldly aspect to which this 'Empire' became attached.

In the second phase of empires we have not only the anointed imperialism of the Church but also the mixture of divine with secular anointing in the Empire. It begins with the ancient Roman Empire in pre-Christian times and continues into the late Middle Ages. Charlemagne was crowned in Rome by the Pope. Externally the kingly dignity becomes a symbol, and thus what is here on earth is no longer a reality. The people of the Middle Ages did not revere Charlemagne or Otto I as gods, as would have been the case in ancient times, but they saw them as human emissaries sent by God, whose mission required confirmation. Awareness of this grew ever fainter, of course. But although it became externalized it nevertheless retained a kind of symbolic reality through its symbols. Thus Stephen I[6] was made King of Hungary by the Pope in the year 1000. A secular ruler is anointed and thus given power by an ecclesiastical or spiritual ruler. What entered into people's consciousness because of this made them believe that there was a justification for drawing others into this Empire which had received its anointing from the gods by means of human beings. Even Dante held the view that the Emperor had the right to rule the whole world.[7]

The myths and legends that crystallize historical events in people's consciousness tend to express things that must be viewed from various angles. Thus in the eleventh or twelfth century there was a strong awareness in Europe that in the Orient long ago human beings who were actually gods had lived on the physical earth. People thought that such gods could no longer live on the earth because it had grown so wicked. What made gods of human beings had been lost. The Holy Grail had been lost, so that now, in the Middle Ages, it could only be attained in the way Perceval attained it, by seeking an inner path to God. Now the empire had become a collection of tokens and symbols, and the God had to be found out of the tokens and symbols.

Thus remnants remain of everything that has ever existed. As long as things are realities they are clear in the world, but later they become ambiguous. As long as the Holy Roman Empire of the German Nation signified one clear-cut thing in people's consciousness, its representative was powerful and capable of keeping in check the various angel-symbols — in other words, the regional princes. People knew that this was his right. But this right rested to a great extent on something that was an idea, and this gradually lost its single meaning. What remained were the regional princes. The awareness that earthly men are sent by God is lost. And the thing that expresses the inability to think that earthly men are sent by God is Protestantism, which is the protest against the real significance of earthly men being sent by God. If the principle of Protestantism had been carried through to its logical conclusion, no crowned or princely head would ever again have been able to claim a position 'by the grace of God'. But remnants remained until 1918; the German regional princes were still there as an external appearance, but they had been meaningful only in those olden times when they stood as symbols for a kingdom of heaven bestowing inspiration.

Similarly, other remnants also remain, and no one realizes that they are remnants. Not so very long ago a Central European bishop — or perhaps he was an archbishop — wrote a pastoral letter[8] in which he implied that a Catholic priest is mightier than Jesus Christ, for the simple reason that when a Catholic priest celebrates the transubstantiation at the altar, Christ Jesus is obliged to be present in the sacred host. The transubstantiation is accomplished by the might of the priest whose actions force Christ Jesus to be present on the altar. The priest, not Christ Jesus, is the stronger because it is he who carries out the transubstantiation on the altar!

To understand this, we have to go back, not to the second phase of imperialism but to the first. Manifold remnants of the first phase of imperialism have been preserved in the Catholic church and its various offices. Thus there is a remnant of the awareness that those who rule on earth are gods, whereas Christ Jesus is only the son of God. And of course from the Protestant point of view this is just as much an impossibility as it is to believe that thousands of years ago human beings regarded a ruler as a god. All these things are real facts that have played their part in historical reality.

It is not so much the opinions that remain, as the customs and habits that arise out of those opinions. Look at the way Islam spread. Muhammad confined himself to saying: 'There is one God, and Muhammad is his prophet.' Thus he took on the role of having been sent by god, which is in keeping with the second phase of imperialism. And yet Islam spread in a manner belonging to the first phase. Muslims have never been as intolerant towards people of other faiths as have those for whom a creed is paramount; they have been quite content merely to conquer other people and make them into subjects, while leaving them to their own beliefs. Thus Islam spread in accordance with the customs of the first phase of imperialism.

Another remnant from the first phase of imperialism, strongly coloured by the second, is Russian despotism, tsarism. In the whole way in which those who recognized the tsar thought about him there is a mood of soul that reaches back to the first phase. That is why it did not much matter in Russia that the forces inherent in the consciousness of the Russian people began to grow towards all that emanated from tsarism, for the power of tsarism actually rested on the Germanic and Mongol elements and not on the element of the Russian peasantry as such. Here again, we have remnants from earlier times.

Now let us come to the third form of imperialism. Its formulation only dates from the present century, at about the time when Chamberlain and his colleagues coined the term 'Imperial Federation'.[9] But its origins lie further back, in the second half of the seventeenth century, when the revolution took place in England which led to that tremendous turnabout that affected all western regions where there were Anglo-American populations. The figure of the king, who had once been a god before becoming one who was merely anointed, degenerated to a mere shadow. Less, even, than a decoration, he was merely tolerated.

Then, from the seventeenth century onwards, the public 'will' passed on to the shoulders of the population as a whole, even though this was at first still layered in social classes. The preconditions brought by the Anglo-American peoples to this 'will' of the people — this election system arising from the people — are different from those brought, for example, by the French. The Latin people, and especially the French, certainly went through their revolution in the eighteenth century. And yet there is an influence which makes the French people more royalist as a nation than any other.[10] It is a matter of the mood within people's souls, and the mutual feeling of unity of the French, their feeling of being a complete nation, is most certainly a very real remnant of their consciousness of Louis XIV.

The English-speaking peoples, however, brought something different. Gradually what asserted itself as public judgement, public opinion, really began to emanate from the elected people in the parliaments. And thus the third form of imperialism developed, formulated later by Chamberlain, for example, and by others. Today we shall consider what this means in terms of the mood in people's souls.

The first empires possessed realities; a human being was the god in the consciousness of the other human beings. In the second empires, what existed on the earth was a token, a symbol; the god merely influenced human beings. And in the third form of empire what comes from human souls is denuded even of the character of a token or symbol. The step was taken from token or symbol to empty words.

Since the seventeenth century what arises in the public life of the Anglo-American peoples, what is spoken about, what is fabricated in the books of law, is indeed the will of the people — even though this is layered in social classes — but it is empty words, from which all substance has been squeezed. And only underneath the squeezed-out, empty words do we find what goes on as reality. No one has any idea that this reality might be divine, or that at least its origin might be divine. Majority decisions obviously cannot lead to anything real; they lead to domination by empty words. Underneath these float the realities, which are not in any way seen as anything divine.

Take one of the important realities that took place: colonization. The 'Imperial Federation' is the form, the particular structure, that the colonial system, the spreading of the Empire to the colonies, has come to have. But how did the colonies originally become attached to the Empire? Think of what really happened. Adventurers, considered rather undesirable at the heart of the Empire, perhaps because they are a bit down at heel, head for the colonies, where they make their fortune. Back home they begin to spend their fortune, but are still not highly regarded; they are still seen as adventurers and bohemians. The realities we now have remain as remnants of the adventurous exploits perpetrated by colonists of somewhat unsavoury repute. The father, perhaps, 'acquired' something out there. His son has a somewhat better reputation; he smells a little better. And his grandson smells even better, so that we come to a time when everything smells very nice indeed. And then empty words take over the thing that is beginning to smell nice. The state takes everything under its wing, becomes the protector, and now everything is done in an honest way.

It would be good if we could call things by their proper name, but the proper name very rarely denotes the actual reality. So instead we must get hold of the things themselves. Only by doing this shall we come to understand the tasks and the responsibilities laid on human beings today by the times in which we live. Only by doing this shall we come to grasp what an artificial convention is the thing we call history, which is perpetrated in schools and universities. History certainly does not call things by their proper name.

I have, you will agree, just described something very terrible. But now what we have to do is to turn with our feelings and emotions towards the responsibilities. So let us take the other side of the coin. When we look at one of those ancient empires we are looking at something real, here on earth: the priest-king emerging from the Mysteries. The second empire was a symbol. The divine jewels with which the rulers and their princes in the ancient oriental empires adorned themselves were a far cry from the third or second or first-class medals of the 'Order of the Eagle', black or red, which are awarded to people in later days. And now reality has become a nothing, for finally the general system of empty words spreading from the West over the rest of the world has taken hold of public affairs.

In the first phase physical reality was thought of as spirit, whereas in future the spirit will have to be actually present here in the physical world. Side by side with physical reality must live spiritual reality. People must go about here, within physical reality, and they must recognize a spiritual reality, they must speak about something genuinely supersensible and invisible that is, however, present here amongst us. It must find a foothold amongst us. Into the space provided by empty words the empire of the spirit must now enter. Everything old has deteriorated into empty words, and by this very means an empty space has been created into which the empire of the spirit is to enter.

In the Anglo-American world, there will continue to be much talk in the usual phrases about all kinds of things that have come down from the past. This will roll on like an unstoppable ball. Especially in the West you find countless formulations that have lost every last scrap of meaning and yet are still in use. Indeed, in everything described in words that are old there lives that wordy emptiness out of which all reality has been squeezed. And here is the space in which the spirit, something that has nothing whatsoever to do with anything old, can take its place. Something entirely new must enter, something that can only spread out as the world of the spirit.

Only then can a kingdom of Christ come into being on the earth. In this kingdom there must be a reality: 'My kingdom is not of this world.' In the kingdom of this world in which the kingdom of Christ first spread, there was still a great deal belonging to this world that had not become empty words. But in the West, in the Anglo-American world, everything to do with human tradition will turn into empty words. So the responsibility is to place a spirit into the vessel that has become empty, a spirit about which it can be said: This kingdom is not of this world! That is the great responsibility. It does not matter how a certain situation has come about. What matters is what is then done with what has come about.

Underneath the surface, particularly in western countries, there are some very effective secret societies who are endeavouring to push the second phase of imperialism into the third phase in a traditional way. In the Anglo-American peoples you have two imperialisms that are intermingled: the economic imperialism of someone like Chamberlain, and the symbolic imperialism of the secret societies, which is very effectively being pushed into the former while being kept hidden from the majority of the people.

LECTURE SIX

Dornach, 21 February 1920

Yesterday, the main thing I wanted you to understand was the way in which present phenomena, that were once real facts, are now actually nothing more than remnants from ancient days. In olden times the institutions and customs in question were realities and still possessed great significance, but these realities have come to an end.

Today we are living in the age of the empty word, and the time has come for us to see how even empty words need a kind of soil on which they can grow, and how on the other hand they are a preparation for something that is to enter into human evolution. If ancient realities did not gradually become illusions it would be impossible for new realities to come into being. Nothing new would come about if, for example, we still had in our time a visible, sense-perceptible god in human form such as existed even in the final days of the ancient Roman empire. Even Nero was still presumed to be a real god in human form. But these things have lost their meaning.

The more things become empty words, the more the soil is prepared for a spiritual, cultural life which is drawn from the supersensible world, a cultural life which seeks divine, spiritual beings not in human form but as real, existing beings amongst the visible human beings here on earth. If we want to comprehend the rather unpalatable conditions of our present time we must be prepared to recognize empty words for what they are, and then turn our attention to the birth of a new cultural, spiritual life.

It is perfectly natural that people want to cling to the old realities, because once they begin to see that things have become empty words they begin to feel uncertain in their hearts and minds. They prefer to delude themselves, because when they do recognize the delusion for what it is, they feel that they are floating up in the air. They will only lose this feeling once they can really begin to sense the stability of the new cultural, spiritual life. We shall have to become participants in the demise of empty words and in the rise of the cultural life of the spirit. In particular this will become possible if English-speaking peoples come to realize more and more that the traditions they have preserved from former times, and which they still talk about so much, are now empty words, whereas the reality underneath these is the economic life.

A moment will come, a moment of extreme importance. People will come to sense how meaningless it is for human beings to stand in physical life as if this were the only reality. Western nations in particular must gradually come to realize this. The moment must come when we admit that we can no longer hold on to anything expressed in words, so that the only reality left for us is our stomach. The necessary admission will not be made until we recognize empty words for what they are, and until we know that the economic life is the only reality. Then, once this admission has been made, human nature will no longer be able to prevent itself from realizing that in order to be human beings we need a spiritual reality in addition to the physical reality of what is only the economic life. This moment of truth must dawn, for without it human evolution cannot proceed.

The strongest flair and talent for this knowledge is to be found among the western nations. Among western nations all the preconditions are right for the dawning of this knowledge, whereas in other European nations there is little aptitude for the dawning of such knowledge with the necessary intensity. In these countries many other conditions prevent people from seeing through their illusions as fundamentally and radically as this can be done in the English-speaking nations. You need only look at historical situations to understand this.

Consider how the various Germanic tribes in Central Europe have been united in the Holy Roman Empire of the German Nation since the time of Charlemagne's heirs. This Empire was fundamentally nothing more than a network of symbols. In everything they faced, people needed to go back from the symbols to some kind of reality, but they failed to reach a full spiritual reality because they were prevented from doing so by the churches. They only got as far as being able to float and swim in a spiritual reality. Therefore everything that the Middle Ages and its successors in the various European confessions had to say about a spiritual reality has the character of something that has been only half understood. It is like the coloured light that shines through the stained-glass windows of medieval churches. People recoiled from a clear and sharply-defined understanding, and preferred to let things stand as something only half known, something that knowledge could not penetrate.

A similar situation governed social relationships. Anyone studying the history of the Holy Roman Empire — and also that of Switzerland, which was closely bound up with it — will find one ambiguity after another being perpetuated from one age to another. The whole thing lost the capacity to endure because, in the end, no one could find any further meaning behind the symbols. And the people of Central Europe were left with a striving and a will that actually contained little of any concrete significance.

This is why in 1870/1 it came to the founding of the Reich with its in-built contradiction. A German Emperor was created on the basis of conditions that were not real. The title was invented. In order to understand what developed in Central Europe you have to realize that history ought not to be studied on the basis of abstract concepts, but on the basis of realities. You have to remember that in history there can be a phenomenon and that underneath this phenomenon there is something else. Once the first phenomenon disappears, because it is an illusion, the second thing can subsequently appear in its real form.

Instead of analysing, one has to point to what is real and concrete. The thing that evolved underneath the German Reich from 1871 until 1914 did not show at that time because that Reich was an illusion. The reality comes afterwards, and this is what has been unfolding since November 1918. That reality is: those who are now in power. The character of what was developing underneath the reign of Kaiser Wilhelm is typified by Noske.[1] It only became possible to explain the German ex-Kaiser once the revolutionary factions now in power made their appearance. The conditions that existed underneath the surface in the preceding decades, when everyone was indulging in illusions, are now the conditions that are present in reality.

This is the real way to study history. You have to look for involution in evolution by searching for what is developing underneath the surface. What is the real name for what called itself Russian tsarism in the nineteenth century? The name for Russian tsarism, now that it has appeared in reality, is Lenin and Trotsky[2] — Bolshevism. This is the concrete reality of what then was a mere illusion. Tsarism is nothing more than the lie swimming on the surface. But what that tsarism was really cultivating appeared in its true reality at the moment when tsarism was swept away. Lenin is nothing other than the tsar. Once his skin had been peeled off, what remained was the reality which today is called Lenin or Trotsky.

Studying history is not a matter of illustrating a phenomenon by means of abstract concepts and ideas but of demonstrating what are historical realities. The definition of a fact in history will always be another fact, not an abstract concept. We must study realities and pay attention to them, for today we are living in an age when realities have to be unearthed and unstintingly revealed.

This is particularly obvious when you study the constitution and content of those secret societies that are exercising a great deal of power in the English-speaking world, a power of which the general public has no inkling. These societies gather together under the most sympathetic of external regulations, and they have gained more and more power during the fifth post-Atlantean period.

You will discover in the England of 1720 only a small number of adherents of these societies. But look at the statistics now. Lodges of Freemasons — in other words societies that make good tools in the hands of the secret societies — number 488 in London, 1354 in the whole of Great Britain, and 486 that are either in the colonies or count as English lodges abroad. Then there are the Royal Arch lodges — 836 of them the world over — which make a secret even of the more external practices of Freemasonry. Let us look first at the content and substance of what lives within these lodges — for these are the tools which those other powers wield.

The content and substance of Freemasonry goes as far back as the ancient first stage of imperialism when the god walked about among human beings, clothed in human form. At that distant time there was a meaning in the content that is now spoken and, in particular, shown in these lodges, but this meaning disappeared long ago. The symbols, however, remain, so that now, especially in English-speaking regions and those dependent on them, there are two layers of cultural 'yeast' working side by side: We have external, exoteric empty words in public life being expressed in ordinary human language and, for example, haunting the parliaments. And we have the secret societies playing about with symbols about which as a rule even those to whom they are handed down understand nothing. It is important to note that side by side with the purely external empty words we also have ceremonial empty words and that these do contain a certain spiritual element.

Indeed, in secret societies that carry on ceremonial forms going back to genuine customs and practices, it can happen that certain individuals, whose karma makes this possible, can discover the real meaning of these symbols. If this happens they are excluded from the societies in question and steps are taken to ensure that they can do no more harm, for the most important thing for these societies is power, not insight. They preserve the secrets in a traditional form, and in this traditional form they have a certain power. Why?

The substance and content are attached to the people who are banded together in these secret societies. One of the more important aspects under which people are banded together there is the refusal to use religious creed as a criterion. This aspect is sinned against nowadays, so that there are, for example, lodges that refuse to accept Jews as members. But such lodges fail to understand the fundamental principle, which is that they ought to embrace people of every creed, and take no account of people's personal beliefs. Another principle in the lodges is that no account should be taken of people's external social origins or other differences. This principle is also sinned against nowadays, for most lodges do not accept members from the working class, but take in only lords and those who dance attendance on them. That this happens does not, however, alter the basic principle of all the members of a lodge being united as brothers. There are the degrees, but these have nothing to do with people's external social class.

People are banded together, then, in accordance with aspects that have nothing whatever to do with the external social order, for in external society itself there are actually quite definite divisions according to creed; and it cannot be claimed that people are all brothers either, for they are not.

Such things are not a matter of indifference. If people of a single creed gather together to form a society, then in real life this society is likely to have only external influence of a kind that is dead. But if people gather together in accordance with the principle that personal beliefs are not in question, then that society will be one that is particularly powerful spiritually. That is why the Catholic church, wishing to gather people together under a more or less uniform creed, has always had to underpin its power by political means. It has always been at its most powerful when the hierarchy, or Rome, has set least store by uniformity of creed. In external life, in ordinary, physical society, to make creed the criterion is equivalent to making oneself powerless. A society can only have power if it attaches no importance to people's individual beliefs.

This is particularly important today, when side by side with public empty words there are also what might be called the esoteric empty words of the ceremonial cult. This is the true origin of today's social confusion. And there are some strange witnesses to the credibility of empty words nowadays.

You will remember that up to the middle of the nineteenth century there were two opposing parties in the English parliament, a liberal party called the Whigs, and a conservative party called the Tories.

But what did these names signify? The name Whig started out as a term of abuse used by the English for Scottish Presbyterians. Later on, perfectly honourable Liberals came to be called Whigs, with no hidden connotations of abuse. And the name Tory came from Ireland where in the seventeenth or eighteenth century it denoted a Papist outlaw. Yet, later on, this term of abuse came to be the official name for English Conservatives. All this went on in the realm of empty words. Reality had nothing to do with it. And wherever you look, first in the English-speaking world and later wherever its influence spread, you will find this going on.

But what does it mean that so many people band together in the lodges in accordance with aspects that are perfectly praiseworthy? It is extremely significant that people gather together in accordance with these most potent aspects, and that there they meet in the ceremonial of the empty words, which in turn joins them together on the basis of a real spiritual foundation. Is it not so that a powerful minister needing an under-secretary of state will prefer to choose a brother Mason rather than anyone else who might come along? Indeed, he is quite justified in making such a choice, since he knows him better and can work more fruitfully with him. A banding-together of this kind is perfectly justifiable and not at all unfavourable for the situation in which it originated. But people will now have to stop working in this way.

What is it that is going on here? It is rather remarkable that in the age of empty words that hold sway in public life there should appear a spiritual community with decidedly effective principles! This spiritual community is very secretive, not so much as regards its membership as with regard to its actual internal intentions. Why is this happening? It is happening because empty words make it possible to falsify realities. What is it that is being created and is, indeed, already in existence? It is an isolated economic life that no longer coincides with the empty word, it is a cultural life that is carried on underneath the surface, and it is a life of rights that strides along dressed up in empty words as though in a toga. As jurisprudence it has about as much significance for the outside world as an English judge sitting there in all his robes.

We have a threefold organization in the realm of empty words, a threefold ordering of untruth. And here is the proof of the need for a genuinely threefold society. To want a threefold ordering of society is the same as to want to replace lies and empty words with truth, with truth which is reality. A period has just begun, however, in which reality is not truth. Empty words can be made to flourish very well in the cultural sphere and also in the sphere of rights and state. But in the economic sphere they are not of much use.

When I give public lectures I describe how, by following the suggestions made in my book *Knowledge of the Higher Worlds*, people can come to develop an inner view of the spiritual world and spiritual reality. But after every third lecture somebody is sure to stand up and say: 'That is all very well, but how is one to know that what one is seeing is a reality? This spiritual world could be nothing but auto-suggestion! It can happen that by merely thinking about lemonade you get a taste of it in your mouth.' In reply to this I always say that it is a matter of whether you are standing fully within reality. Of course you can suggest to yourself the taste of lemonade, but your thirst remains unquenched. If you take things far enough you will find that they do lead to reality. You cannot, with any success, have empty words in the economic sphere, because you cannot eat them, or at any rate your hunger cannot be satisfied by them. So of all the realities, the reality of the economic sphere is the one that has characteristically remained behind.

The moment we recognize the illusion for what it is, and the empty word for what it is, we will be overcome by a feeling of immense shame. We will discover that we human beings, endowed as we are with intelligence, use this intelligence purely to take care of the economic basis of our physical life, which is something the animals do without the benefit of intelligence. If, as human beings, we use our intelligence for nothing other than taking care of our economic life by providing food and everything else we need for our physical existence, then we are prostituting our intelligence, because we are using it to do something which the animals can perfectly well do without possessing the luxury of an intelligence. At the moment when this self-knowledge dawns on us, at the moment when we see empty words for what they are, we shall see the beginning of a great feeling of shame. And then the turnround will come. Then will come the realization that a renewal of spirit and culture is needed.

Suitable preparation will have to be made for this by ensuring that a sufficiently large number of people can see the situation of today as it really is. What is the point of indulging in illusions about how things really stand? What is the point of believing in Lloyd George[3] when you can see perfectly well that whatever comes out of his mouth cannot be anything but empty words? Why bother to consider the situation in Europe on the basis of principles which have for centuries been inherited from ancient times and which can have no potential for the conditions of today?

Historical phenomena ought to be recognized for what they symbolize. It is time we realized that notable things are expressed by external appearances. Take the Habsburgs. They originated in Alsace and travelled slowly eastwards via Switzerland until they reached their most easterly point as the apostolic Kings of Hungary. The remarkable thing is that western realities dwindle when they go eastwards. The Hohenzollerns made a shorter journey, only from Nuremberg to Berlin, but it was also from West to East. These historical symptoms are genuine symbols to which attention must be paid.

Equally we must pay attention to the realities that lie underneath the empty words. That is why it is impossible today to discover any reality in public opinion. If you have a sense for what is real you come up against the most extraordinary things. You can try to get to the bottom of things that occur in public life and are imitated and emulated all over the world, such as the Whigs and the Tories. You go back to their beginnings and find that they were terms of abuse and that people later had to take them seriously because no other fitting names could be found for the realities they represented. In public life today we endeavour to shroud words in a kind of mystical gloom without realizing we are doing so.

For example, I know of a book that is a code of nothing but empty words. You can open it anywhere and come across the most peculiar sentences such as: The law is the will of a people. But today 'people' means nothing more than a collection of individuals. And this collection is supposed to have a will! All the explanations in this book are like this. This code of empty words is entitled *The State* and its author is Woodrow Wilson.[4] It was, of course, not Wilson's intention to permit himself the luxury of making an anthology of all the empty words at present current in public life; but that is what he in fact succeeded in doing. This shows how the way people think and speak in empty words has little to do with any reality.

Without getting to the bottom of these things, without paying full attention to the reality in these things wherever we find them, we can make no progress today. Little thoughts will get us nowhere, so we must pluck up our courage to think great thoughts.

LECTURE SEVEN

Dornach, 22 February 1920

Something that belongs to the very nature of imperialism will become clear to you on going over the lectures of yesterday and the day before. This is, that a community that is imperialistic will tend to perpetuate in an automatic way certain things that were once its understandable, though not always justifiable, tasks. If a community needs to defend itself for a while, this is perfectly justifiable. The necessary professions will be created, such as those of the police or the military. But when the danger has passed the people involved want to go on working in their professions, and so something is perpetuated that can no longer be explained in the context of the new reality. It can even happen that what was originally founded for the purpose of defence develops an aggressive character of its own. This can happen in every stage of imperialism except the very first, where justification for extending dominion over others lay in the people's awareness that their ruler was god. An impetus to spread dominion over others was not inbuilt in subsequent imperialisms; it came about for other reasons.

In earliest times it was the will of the ruler, who was a divine being, that was the indisputable power factor. Therefore, in the public life of those earliest empires there was nothing to discuss, since the fact that the ruler was a god, walking on the earth in human form, provided a safe and secure foundation on which to order public and social affairs. In the first stage of imperialism you cannot really speak at all about what today we term 'rights'. You cannot discuss things like institutions of the state. The only thing you can talk about is the manifestation of divine power through physical human beings. It is meaningless to discuss whether the god in human form ought or ought not to do what he does. And there was indeed no such discussion in those most ancient times.

But then comes the time when we are expected to see in the physical situation merely the image of the spiritual world. We speak of what Saint Augustine[1] called the 'City of God', a state here on earth that is an image of heavenly facts and heavenly personalities. When this time comes it is possible for one individual to regard what the representative of the divine is doing as correct — a true image of the divine — while another individual can dispute this and say that it is not a proper image. It becomes possible to enter into discussion. Criticizing and discussing does not come about until the second stage; not until that stage does it become possible to form a judgement of one's own, to add a predicate to a subject. Gradually, a thing such as the kind of parliament we have today could come into existence. There is no point in having a parliament if there is no way of discussing public affairs. In other words, even the most primitive form of public discussion is a characteristic of the second stage.

But today we live in the third stage. What is characteristic for western countries has spread, more or less, over the whole world. In the stage of the empty word the inner substance of discussion has disappeared, and therefore everyone can be right, or at least can imagine that he is right. It is impossible to demonstrate to him that he is wrong, because any claim can be made, anything can be asserted.

However, earlier stages are always perpetuated in those that follow them, and out of this arise the inner impulses for imperialisms. People are so superficial in the observations they make. If a former German Emperor can express his opinion by writing 'The will of the king is the loftiest law', it means that in the age of empty words he is saying something that only has meaning in the first stage. But legal concepts, in which discussion — putting forward and pleading a case — is intrinsic, can only be understood in their reality in the context of the second stage.

There is something in legal concepts as such that is irridescent, because they belong to the age of symbols, in which what is spiritual shines and shimmers through the material world. So if you are confronted only with the external signs — as they can exist in legal words and legal customs — you can then argue and discuss about what is legal and right. Indeed, in public life as such, you can put forward cases and argue about what are rights.

But in the age of empty phrases there is no longer any understanding of the need to look at what is actually there in the social situation before laying down a concept of what law is. Here law is defined in the way I quoted yesterday, giving the example of Woodrow Wilson. You have to imagine a person so strongly bound up in abstract idealism, not to say materialism — for the two are very alike — that he can say: Law is the will of the state. Even to be tempted to say or write down such a thing you have to have taken leave of any capacity to look at things as they really are.

In the third stage, as we have seen, we are concerned with economic life as the essential reality. The age of the empty word is definitely necessary for the course of evolution, so that empty words which have no content may open people's eyes to the fact that the only reality they have all around them is economic life, and they now have to spread real culture, the new spirit, all over the world.

Notions about this new cultural spirit are as yet exceedingly meagre, and it is perfectly understandable that it should still be surrounded by the most preposterous misunderstandings; yet it will eventually have to penetrate to the very roots of human life. I explained yesterday how in matters of substance and content the secret societies preserve ancient things in a way that is merely traditional. But despite this, in their external slogan of 'brotherliness' — in the sense of not taking account of either class distinctions or personal beliefs within the lodges — there is a definite essence that will prepare for the future in the right way, though somewhat differently, as I shall explain in a moment.

I want to use something very ordinary as an example, but it is intended to be taken very seriously. We say: The tree is green. This manner of expressing something belongs firmly in the second stage of human evolution. Imagine having to paint what it is that you express in the judgement: The tree is green. It is, in fact, impossible to paint. You can put green paint on to a surface but you are not painting anything to do with the tree. And if you paint any other parts of the tree, the ones that are not green, this gets in the way even more. If you try to paint 'the tree is green', you are painting something that is dead. The manner in which we join the predicate to the subject is something that can only be used to depict something that is dead in the way we see it in the world. We form judgements such as the statement 'the tree is green' because we have as yet no picture in ourselves of the way in which the world is alive, nor do we know how to express something that lives and weaves. The statement 'the tree is green' presupposes that there is a relationship between something or other and the green colour, whereas in actual fact it is the colour itself that is being creative and is part of the force that is living and weaving. The transformation of human thinking and feeling will have to penetrate into the very depths of soul life, and this will take a long time to come about. But when it does, it will have its effect on the way in which human beings relate to one another.

We are now very much at the beginning of all this, but it is time for us to gain some insight into the pathways that lead towards the light. As I said earlier, something important happens when people associate together in such a way that their personal beliefs are irrelevant. In view of this, I would ask you to consider deeply the manner in which Anthroposophy is described. It is described without definitions and ordinary judgements. Although people do not on the whole realize this as yet, the attempt is always made, in essence, to give pictures, to depict things from many different sides. Virtually the most meaningless thing you can do is endeavour to nail down the insights of spiritual science to something that can be judged in terms of Yes or No. People are still very much inclined to do this, but it is impossible.

Because we are only now beginning to embark on the third stage, there is a misunderstanding that keeps on cropping up. Someone may ask about a particularly difficult problem they are faced with and they may duly receive some advice. And immediately they generalize, assuming that this advice applies to similar situations in life, wherever they may occur. The fact of the matter is, however, that the advice they have received has only a limited application, because judgements based on spiritual insight are individual and apply only to the case in question. This habit of generalizing, that belongs to the second stage of human evolution, must not be allowed to continue on into the future. A way of overcoming these habits, now causing havoc in the soul, is to gain absolute clarity about all aspects of what goes on.

The day before yesterday I suggested that in many ways the Catholic church appears like a shadow of the first stage of human evolution. At certain times this shadowy appearance condensed very strongly into a kind of psychological imperialism, as was the case, for example, with the monks of Cluny, who ruled Europe far more thoroughly in the eleventh century than one might think.[2] Roman Catholic dogma tends to make the priest feel himself to be greater than Christ, because he can force Christ to be present upon the altar. This is a clear indication of the Catholic church as a shadowy appearance of what existed in the most ancient imperialism of all. You know that there is great enmity in the West between the Catholic church and all those societies that use Freemasonry, or at least a particular form of it, as their tool. In these secret societies there is a very strong view of the Catholic church as a shadowy image of the first stage that has meanwhile come to an end. Charlemagne and the Ottos had themselves crowned by the Pope, thus using what had remained of the first imperialisms as the vessel into which they poured the imperialisms of the second stage.

We, in our turn, have arrived at the third stage, economic imperialism, which is becoming especially visible in the West. Behind the scenes of this economic imperialism there exists the culture of the secret societies who still their hunger with empty symbols. It is clearly seen that the external, social constitution of the church is merely a shadowy image of something that used to exist but which no longer has any significance. But with regard to the second stage the situation is not yet understood. Hence the great illusion in which the statesmen of the western world still find themselves. Woodrow Wilson would no longer speak of the will of the church, but the will of the state is something he takes for granted.

The state as the bearer of rights, however, only enjoyed during the second stage of human evolution the significance still assigned to it today. At present, everything new is being poured into the state, just as in the Middle Ages everything new was poured into the church. Everything that has come together in the concept of freedom is poured into the state. And everything that belongs to the economic imperialism of Great Britain is poured into the state, so that those who are brought up in Great Britain, well-intentioned though their education may be, come to see the state as something that can be taken for granted and which can quite well be assumed to have a will of its own.

People must come to recognize that retaining the state — a body of rights and legal institutions — as the overall framework of the social organism, into which all other institutions have to be fitted, is just as much a perpetuation of shadows as is the case with the church. Few people understand this as yet. You need only consider how almost everything people are enthusiastic about in public affairs is squeezed into the concept of the state. For nationalists and chauvinists everything thought of as belonging to the nation, national chauvinism, is incorporated into the state, in order to construct the concept of the nation state. Socialism too, even radical socialism, is seen in the framework of the state. People have no notion of the fact that this is destined to become a shadowy image.

In some Protestant circles it is now understood that the church is only an external institution, and that what is essentially religious has to find its roots in human hearts. But this stage has nowhere yet been reached with regard to the concept of the state, as is obvious in the way people are seeking to squeeze all kinds of nationalisms into the new European structure of states brought about by the recent hostilities.

All these attitudes fail to take heed of the fact that whatever comes about in the course of human history is something living, and not a mechanism. Whatever is alive goes through growth and decay, but this does not fit in with the imperialistic view, which involves no thought for the future. In public life today the thoughts that exist about the future are dead thoughts, not living ones. People think that something they institute today will be fine and will then continue to exist forever. The women's movement thinks like this, and so does socialism, and so does nationalism: We are going to set something up; everything has been waiting for us to become clever enough; now we have discovered the cleverest thing for all eternity, so it will continue in existence for all eternity. This is like bringing up a child until he is eighteen and then saying: I have made a good job of his education and from now on he will remain as he is. The fact, however, is that he will grow older and he will also die, and it is the same with everything that comes into being in human evolution.

This brings us to what I mentioned earlier about there being something further that must be added to the principle of taking no account of personal beliefs and the principle of brotherly love amongst human beings. The thing that must be added is a living attitude that includes death, in its reckoning for life here on earth. We must come to understand that we institute things in the present that will one day have to pass away again, because they bear the principle of death within them from the beginning, lack any desire to go on forever, and have no intention of being permanent.

How will it be possible to do such a thing? Certainly not under the influence of the way people thought in the second stage. But it will be possible when that feeling of shame sets in about which I spoke yesterday. When we begin to realize that we are living in the empire of the empty word, underneath which the sole reality that glimmers is economic imperialism, then people will begin to call out for a knowledge of the spirit that speaks of it as an invisible kingdom, a kingdom that is not of this world, and therefore one in which the Christ-impulse can truly begin to finds its place.

This can only begin if society is ordered in a threefold way; if the economic life is administered separately; if, in the life of rights, the state is no longer an absolute, all-embracing concept, but something which deals solely with those things that really belong to the sphere of rights; and if the spiritual, cultural sphere is truly free to develop a genuine life of the spirit here in the real world. The spirit can only flourish among human beings if it is dependent only upon itself and if all the institutions that cultivate the spirit depend on nothing but themselves.

What is it that will come about when society has been ordered in this threefold way, when society has become an organism? We shall have an economy that lives. It will be just like the original imperialism — everything at work in it will be present within life on the physical earth. In this economic limb of the organism the ordering forces must be taken from the economic life itself. Once society is ordered in the manner described in the book *Towards Social Renewal*[3] I do not think that anyone will imagine that there is anything supersensible taking a direct part in economic life. When we eat or prepare food, when we manufacture clothes, then everything is reality. The aesthetic aspects may be symbolic, but the actual clothes are reality.

And in the second limb of the social organism there will in future be nothing symbolic such as there was in the second stage of human evolution, when the state embodied the all-embracing law. Everything appearing in one human being will be an image of what also lives in the other human being. Out of the present time a new symbolism will be developed, in which what one human being does is always a token of the whole sphere of rights that is being built up.

The third limb will be neither a symbol nor empty words, but spiritual reality. The spirit will be enabled to live in reality among human beings.

In this way, by really going over to inward truthfulness, it will be possible to build up the social order. However, this will be particularly difficult because, although in this age of empty words people acquire the habit of a quite shrewd form of cleverness, this shrewd cleverness is actually nothing but a play with words that stand for old concepts. A typical example of this was when there emerged out of the imperialism of empty words the idea that the King or Queen of England ought also to be given the title of Emperor or Empress of India. All kinds of beautiful reasons can be found for inventing this title, but nothing would have altered if it had never been invented. The Austrian Emperor — until he was no longer an emperor — bore the title of King of Jerusalem. This stemmed from the Crusades. There is no better way of demonstrating the role played by something that says absolutely nothing; it plays a far greater role than anyone might think.

Those who live amid empty words believe they are thinking when they merely take words that stand for ancient concepts and roll them around in their brain. We can only find our way back to real thinking by filling our inner, soul life with substance, and this substance can only come from knowledge of the spiritual world. Only by filling themselves with spiritual life can people become fully human once again, after having been bladders filled with hot air and perfectly satisfied with the empty shells of words.

Out of the feeling of shame that I mentioned yesterday the call for the spirit will arise. And the possibility for the word of the spirit to spread can only come if the cultural life of the spirit can develop in independence. If this cannot happen, our only choice will be to work in tiny patches in the way we had to do in the case of the Waldorf School,[4] which was enabled to come about only because there was a loophole in the education law of Württemberg. What belongs to the life of spirit and culture can only be established out of spirit and culture. What is needed must be brought into play out of the spiritual world, and there must be no interference from the other two spheres.

At present the whole tenor of our time still refuses to reckon with the fact that with every new generation a new spiritual life will ever-increasingly appear on earth. Irrespective of whether totalitarian states or soviet republics are set up, the consequence will be the same if there is no awareness of the fact that everything that comes into being in life is subject to the rules of life, which entail constant change and also death. If we set up administrations that fail to take into account the rule of metamorphosis and change, then we are quite simply making sure that every succeeding generation will be revolutionary. The social organism is a living organism. It can only be seen as something alive if its threefold form is understood.

Those whose favourable economic position allows them to spread an imperialism over virtually the whole world have the heavy, terrible and intense responsibility of making clear to themselves the fact that into this imperialism must be poured a cultivation of true spiritual and cultural life. The hollow mockery of a situation must be sensed in which the British Isles founded an economic empire that spanned the world and then, when seeking profound, mystical spirituality, turned to those they had conquered economically — and are now economically exploiting — in order to glean from them their spirituality. The real obligation is to take one's own spiritual substance and pour it into the outer form of the social organism.

It is an awareness of this that I believe our British friends should take away with them from here. It is the awareness that in this historic moment all those who belong to world-wide organizations in which English is spoken have the responsibility to ensure that real spirituality is brought into the external empire of the economy. The choice is stark. Either the only efforts made are those in the economic realm world-wide — in which case the demise of earthly civilization will be the guaranteed consequence — or spirit must be poured into this economic empire, and then the aims of earthly evolution will be achieved. I would like to suggest that this should be called to mind extremely seriously every morning and that every individual action should be made with this impulse in mind. The hour of world history is striking with great gravity at the present time — with gravity and very terribly. We have reached the culmination of emptiness in words. And now the time has come for us to take into our life of soul and into our social life a content of real substance. We have to realize that this stark choice is waiting to be made by every one of us. With the inmost forces of our soul each one of us has to participate in making this decision. If we do not do so, we are not living in the affairs of mankind.

Yet in this age of empty words there is such longing for illusion. People would so much like to disregard the seriousness of life. They would rather not see the truth that holds sway in what goes on today. The longing for truth must begin to dawn in human beings, and above all the longing for the freeing of spiritual life, and the knowledge that no one has the right to call himself a Christian who cannot understand the words: 'My kingdom is not of this world.'

What this means is that the empire, the kingdom of Christ, must become one that is genuinely invisible, a kingdom about which we speak as we do about invisible things. Not until the science of the spirit holds sway will it be possible to speak of such a kingdom. Neither an external church nor an external state can realize this kingdom, and neither can an empire of the economic sphere. The only thing that can bring this kingdom to realization is the will of the individual human being living in an independent sphere of spirit and culture.

Since we cannot presume that the life of the spirit will be made free in regions where people are now being downtrodden, we must see to it that this is done in regions where, at present, people are not being downtrodden, whether politically, economically or — as the others soon will be — spiritually and culturally. And above all we must be entirely clear about the fact that we have not reached the point at which we can say: Although everything has been going downhill for so long, things will now begin to move upwards again. No such thing will happen unless people themselves begin to act out of the spirit. If they do not, things will continue to deteriorate. A beginning must be made in producing what is needed out of the impulse of the spirit. Meanwhile, the human race continues to live off old reserves which will soon be used up. It is childish and naîve to imagine that once the lowest point is reached things will begin to improve if we sit with our hands in our lap. This will not happen.

Our strongest wish is that words such as these will kindle fires in the souls of those who count themselves as members of the anthroposophical movement. Our wish is that the spectre that haunts so many people — especially, perhaps, those who find their way to this anthroposophical movement — may be conquered by the spirit about which we are speaking here. When individuals find their way to a movement like ours it is understandable that they are seeking something for themselves and for their own soul. And they are welcome to find what they are seeking; but only so that mankind as a whole may be helped by them to make progress. We cannot remind ourselves about this often enough, and this should be added to the other thing which I suggested should be called to mind every morning.

If we had taken the profoundest impulse of our movement more seriously to heart we would have achieved better progress by now. But, unfortunately, much that is done in our circles does not help us towards the future; indeed it often hinders us. It is very important to ask ourselves why this is so. Especially must we not imagine that there will be no opposition from most forceful opponents against any endeavours aimed at the welfare of mankind.

I have mentioned a number of things that are being done against this movement — stumbling blocks of enmity that are being placed in its path. I feel that it is my duty to point these things out to you, so that you are never tempted to feel that one thing or another has been successfully refuted. Nothing can be refuted, because these opponents are not concerned with getting at the truth. They want to take as little account as possible of our actual concerns, and their main purpose is to attack from all sides with slanderous accusations. Slogans are formulated that are intended to do as much harm as possible among those who are susceptible to slogans. But such things point to what most people today would prefer not to see and would rather go on deluding themselves about.

The situation is much worse than one can bring oneself to imagine, and it is extremely important not to misinterpret the seriousness of the times. We have got to realize that we are only at the beginning of the things that will work against the progress of mankind. Without neglecting our responsibility we cannot for one second turn away from what is emerging at this very moment as a fundamental evil at the root of mankind. The very worst that can happen today is to listen to slogans and empty words, and to believe that outdated concepts contain anything that is still rooted in human reality, for the new reality must be called forth out of the fountainhead of the spirit itself.

These, my dear friends, are some of the things I wanted to say to you all today — and in particular to our English friends whose visit here has been a source of great gladness, so that on their return they will have something on which to base their activities precisely where this will be so very important. You will have noticed that the things I have said were not intended either as praise or blame, and that I certainly had no intention of flattering anyone. The things that have been said here have been said for the sake of the truth. I do believe that you have come here in order to hear the truth. From your sojourn you will have learnt that speaking the truth is not a comfortable thing to do nowadays because, now more than ever, the truth calls forth opposition. Do not be afraid of opposition, for to have opponents and to speak the truth is one and the same thing today. You must come to understand these things. And we shall always best understand one another if our mutual understanding is founded on the desire to hear the unvarnished truth.

In this last lecture before my departure for Germany, this is what I wanted to say to you all, and especially to our English friends.

NOTES

LECTURE ONE

1 Rudolf Steiner was about to depart for Stuttgart, a journey for which exit and re-entry visas were required by Switzerland at that time.
2 See Rudolf Steiner *Ways to a New Style in Architecture*, Rudolf Steiner Press, Sussex 1992/3. Also *Der Baugedanke des Goetheanum* (The Idea of the Goetheanum Building), Dornach, Bibliography No. GA 289. Lecture of 29 June 1921.
3 1 Corinthians 3:19. 'For the wisdom of this world is foolishness with God.'
4 Illustrations in *Der Baugedanke des Goetheanum*. See Note 2.
5 See Rudolf Steiner *Von Seelenrätseln* (Riddles of the Soul), Dornach 1983, Bibliography No. GA 21, parts of which are translated in *The Case for Anthroposophy*, Rudolf Steiner Press, London 1970.
6 See lecture of 2 January 1924 in Rudolf Steiner *Principles of Physiology and Therapy in the Light of Spiritual Science*. Available in typescript at Rudolf Steiner House Library, London. No. R 38.

LECTURE TWO

1 See Rudolf Steiner *The Portal of Initiation*, Scene Four.

LECTURE THREE

1 Friedrich Traub *Rudolf Steiner als Philosoph und Theosoph* (Rudolf Steiner as a Philosopher and Theosophist), Tübingen 1919. Rudolf Steiner discussed this pamphlet in his lecture of 16 November 1919 in *Menschliche Verantwortlichkeit — Weltverantwortlichkeit — Menschheitskultur*, Dornach 1951. Before a lecture on 28 November 1919 he made the following comments: 'Let me read you a short article by our friend Dr Stein entitled "Neue Wahlverwandtschaften" (New elective affinities) which appeared in the last issue of *Dreigliederung des sozialen Organismus*: "In the Sieglehaus in Stuttgart on 11 November, a member of the cathedral chapter, Laun, gave an entirely insignificant lecture on the subject of *Theosophy and Christianity*, of which we would have taken no notice had it not been typical of a certain way of thinking which I shall describe. The lecturer's train of thought, or rather the sequence of his sentences, followed exactly the pamphlet by Professor Traub entitled *Steiner als Philosoph und Theosoph*. No mention was made of Traub himself, of course, but the interesting symptom to observe was that the Catholic member of the cathedral chapter was making common cause with the Protestant professor — behind the scenes. The Catholic and Protestant parties (for they are not religions any longer) have joined forces against Steiner. Two parties who are at loggerheads in public are at one behind the scenes. The general tone of the lecturer's weapons may be gauged from the fact that there was no discussion

afterwards, while the lecturer suggested that those seeking more information about Steiner should approach his opponents and not consult his actual writings, since these had been forbidden by the Pope. Dr J. W. Stein.'' (in the journal *Dreigliederung des sozialen Organismus*, Stuttgart, No.21.)

You can see from this how necessary it is to form unprejudiced opinions about our contemporaries, and how inappropriate it has become to assess situations superficially and in isolation, which is unfortunately still often done, even in our circles. It cannot be said often enough that the times are extremely grave and that it is not enough, out of lethargic convenience, merely to perpetuate the old belief in authority in a new form.'

2 Dr Walter Johannes Stein, (Vienna 1891-1957 London). Teacher at the Stuttgart Waldorf School and at Michael Hall Rudolf Steiner School in London, writer and lecturer.

3 See Rudolf Steiner *Weltsilvester und Neujahrsgedanken* (Thoughts on the New Year), Dornach 1962, Bibliography No. GA 195.

4 In the *Canones contra Photium* of this Council, against the patriarch Photius, the 11th canon stipulates that the human being does not possess 'two souls' but '*unam animam rationabilem et intellectualem*'. It was thus conceded, that this one soul did possess some spiritual characteristics.

5 The story referred to may be found in Diogenes Laertius *The Lives and Opinions of Eminent Philosophers*, Book VI, Chapter 2, 'Life of Diogenes', literally translated by C. D. Yonge, London 1853.

6 Rudolf Steiner *The Riddle of Man*, Mercury Press, New York 1990, Bibliography No. GA 20, and *Von Seelenrätseln*, op. cit.

7 Adolf von Harnack (1851-1930), German Protestant church historian. See *What is Christianity? Sixteen lectures 1899-1900 at the University of Berlin*, tr. T. B. Saunders, London 1958.

8 See, for example, Rudolf Steiner *The Challenge of the Times*, Anthroposophic Press, New York 1941, Bibliography No. GA 186.

LECTURE FOUR

1 See particularly Rudolf Steiner *Kosmische und menschliche Geschichte*, 6 volumes, Dornach, various dates (Bibliography Nos. GA 170-174b), parts of which are available in English in *The Riddle of Humanity: the Spiritual Background of Human History*, Rudolf Steiner Press, London 1990; *Inner Impulses of Human Evolution. The Mexican Mysteries and the Knights Templar*, Anthroposophic Press, New York 1984; *The Karma of Vocation*, Anthroposophic Press, New York 1984; *The Karma of Untruthfulness*, Rudolf Steiner Press, London, Vol.1 1988, Vol.2 1992; *The Mission of the Archangel Michael*, Anthroposophic Press, New York 1961, as well as other lectures from 1917 to 1919.

2 See Rudolf Steiner *Towards Social Renewal*, Rudolf Steiner Press, London 1977, as well as volumes mentioned in Note 1 above.

3 See Plato's *Phaedrus*, 242.

4 The Theosophical Society, founded in 1875 in New York, moved its headquarters a few years later to Adyar, near Madras, in India. In her first work *Isis Unveiled*, its founder, H. P. Blavatsky, still adhered to western

occultism, but as time went on she increasingly turned to Indian wisdom. See Rudolf Steiner *The Occult Movement in the Nineteenth Century*, Rudolf Steiner Press, London 1973.

5 John Locke (1632-1704), English philosopher. David Hume (1711-1776), Scottish philosopher, historian, economist and essayist. John Stuart Mill (1806-1873), English philosopher and economist. Herbert Spencer (1820-1903), English philosopher. Charles Robert Darwin (1809-1882), English naturalist, first soundly established the theory of organic evolution in his monumental work *Origin of Species*.

6 Georg Friedrich Wilhelm Hegel (1770-1831), Immanuel Kant (1724-1804), Johann Gottlieb Fichte (1762-1814), Friedrich Wilhelm Joseph von Schelling (1775-1854), the great German philosophers of the eighteenth and nineteenth centuries. See Rudolf Steiner *The Riddles of Philosophy*, Anthroposophic Press, New York 1973, Bibliography No. GA 18, and *The Riddle of Man*, op. cit.

7 Wilhelm von Humboldt (1767-1835), German philologist, diplomat and man of letters. His work *The Sphere and Duties of Government*, tr. J. Cailthard, jun., London 1854, was completed in 1851. A literal translation of the German title would be 'Ideas for an attempt to determine the limits of the sphere of influence of the state'.

8 See Rudolf Steiner *Friedrich Nietzsche. Fighter for Freedom*. Rudolf Steiner Publishers, New Jersey 1960. See also 'David Strauss' in 'Thoughts out of Season', Vol 4 and 5 of *The Complete Works of Friedrich Nietzsche*, The first complete and authorized English translation, ed. Dr Oscar Levy, London 1909.

9 Herman Grimm (1828-1901), German writer. The quotation comes from his essay 'Heinrich von Treitschkes Deutsche Geschichte' in *Beiträge zur deutschen Culturgeschichte*, Berlin 1897.

10 Louis XIV of France (1638-1715).

11 Thomas Woodrow Wilson (1856-1924), 28th President of the United States of America (1913-1921). As head of the Entente, on 8 January 1918, in one of his more important war speeches, he enumerated the Fourteen Points for self-government amongst all the nations of the world, which he regarded as an essential basis of a just and lasting peace.

12 See *The Complete Works of Friedrich Nietzsche*, Volume 1, 'The Birth of Tragedy, or Hellenism and pessimism' (The literal translation of this title: The birth of tragedy out of the spirit of music). (Note 8, above.)

13 *Asuras*: See Rudolf Steiner *Geisteswissenschaftliche Menschenkunde*, Dornach 1979, Bibliography No. GA 107, lecture of 22 March 1909 in Berlin. This lecture is in English translation in *The Deed of Christ and the Opposing Spiritual Powers*, Steiner Book Centre, Vancouver 1976.

LECTURE FIVE

1 Lectures Five to Seven in this collection formed the final three of a longer series of eighteen given by Rudolf Steiner in Dornach between 9 January and 22 February 1920, all of which appear under the German title *Geistige und Soziale Wandlungen in der Menschheitsentwickelung* (Spiritual and

Social Change in Human Evolution), Dornach 1966, Bibliography No. GA 196.

2 See Lecture Four, Note 11. In a public lecture given in Zurich on 12 November 1917, Rudolf Steiner spoke against Wilson who was endeavouring to depict the structure of society in terms of natural science. The difficulties Wilson encountered after his return to the United States meant that the Treaty of Versailles, in the formulation of which Wilson had played such a decisive part, was not in the end ratified by the United States of America. In the autumn of 1920 the Republican Warren Harding was elected President with a landslide majority.

3 The 'Imperial Federation League' was founded in England in 1884, but could never unite on a single policy. The imperialism of a 'Greater Britain' as a power to be reckoned with emerged particularly at the beginning of the twentieth century under the influence of Joseph Chamberlain (1836-1906).

4 Four treatises of Dionysius the Areopagite are extant: 'Divine Names', 'Mystical Theology', 'Celestial Hierarchy' and 'Ecclesiastical Hierarchy'. The last two complement one another.

5 Charles IV, crowned in Rome in 1355, set out to make the Holy Roman Empire a specifically German institution. He defined the rights of the electors in the Golden Bull of 1356 and the changes he made were reflected in the final evolution of the empire's title: *Sacrum Romanum imperium nationis Germanicae* (the Holy Roman Empire of the German Nation).

6 Stephen I (St Stephen) of Hungary (997-1038). After successfully putting down a pagan insurrection, he completed the Christianization of the Hungarians, begun by his father Géza, against much opposition from pagan nobles, bringing stability to state and church alike. He was canonized in 1083.

7 Dante's formula of a universal empire: 'The human race, therefore, is ordered well, nay, is ordered for the best, when according to the utmost of its power it becomes like unto God. But the human race is most like unto God when it is most one, for the principle of unity dwells in Him alone... The human race is most one when all are united together, a state which is manifestly impossible unless humanity as a whole becomes subject to one Prince...' *The De Monarchia of Dante Alighieri*, edited with translation and notes by Aurelia Henry, Boston, New York and Cambridge, 1904.

8 Pastoral letter of Archbishop Katschthaler of Salzburg dated 2 February 1905, quoted in Carl Mirbt *Quellen zur Geschichte des Papsttums und des römischen Katholizismus* (Documentations for a history of the Papacy and Roman Catholicism), Tübingen 1934, p.228.

9 See Note 3 above.

10 Lecture of 15 February 1920 in *Geistige und Soziale Wandlungen in der Menschheitsentwickelung*, op. cit. See also Lecture Four, Note 10.

LECTURE SIX

1 Gustav Noske (1868-1946), wood-worker; later, editor of social-democrat newspapers. In November 1918 he quelled the mutiny in the fleet in Kiel.

On 6 January 1919 he became commander-in-chief of all troops in Berlin and on 13 February 1919 was made Minister of Defence of the Reich, an appointment he retained until 30 March 1920.

2 Lenin (1870-1924), founder of bolshevik communism and the greatest single driving force behind the Soviet revolution of October-November 1917. Trotsky (1879-1940), a Soviet political leader and chief organizer of the Red Army. Later Stalin's most conspicuous victim.

3 David Lloyd George (1863-1945), British Prime Minister from 1916 to 1922.

4 Woodrow Wilson *The State: Elements of Historical and Practical Politics*, Boston 1889.

LECTURE SEVEN

1 St Augustine of Hippo (354-430), *De civitate Dei*. He is generally recognized as the greatest thinker of Christian antiquity.

2 The abbey of Cluny was founded in AD 910. A great network of monasteries following the Cluniac custom and looking to Cluny for the maintenance of discipline was gradually built up in every country.

3 Rudolf Steiner *Towards Social Renewal*, op. cit.

4 The first Rudolf Steiner (Waldorf) school was founded in Stuttgart, Württemberg, in 1919.